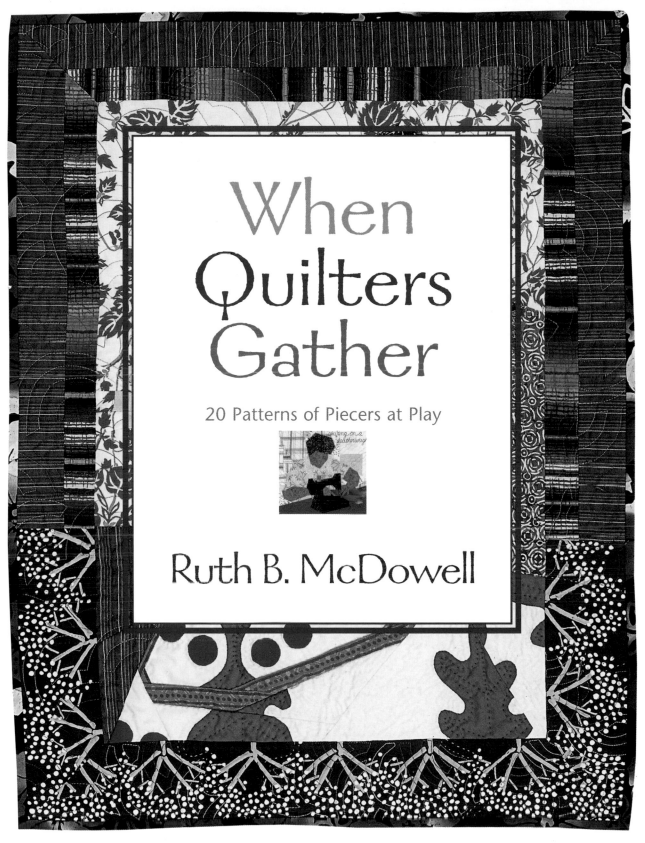

When Quilters Gather

20 Patterns of Piecers at Play

Ruth B. McDowell

C&T PUBLISHING

© 2003, Ruth B. McDowell

Editor-in-Chief: Darra Williamson

Editor: Lynn Koolish

Technical Editors: Karyn Hoyt-Culp,
Diane Kennedy-Jackson

Copyeditors: Ellen Pahl, Eva Simoni Erb

Proofreader: Susan Nelsen

Cover Designer: Christina Jarumay

Design Director: Diane Pedersen

Book Designer: Jill K. Berry

Illustrator: Kate Reed

Production Assistant: Kirstie L. McCormick

Photography: David Caras unless
otherwise noted

How-to Photography: Diane Pedersen and
Gailen Runge

Published by C&T Publishing, Inc., P.O. Box
1456, Lafayette, California, 94549

Library of Congress Cataloging-in-Publication
Data

McDowell, Ruth B.
  When quilters gather : 20 patterns of piecers
at play / Ruth B.
McDowell.
    p. cm.
  ISBN 1-57120-212-9 (paper trade)
  1. Patchwork—Patterns. 2. Quilting—
Patterns. I. Title.
  TT835.M245 2003
  746.46—dc21

                            2002155443

Printed in China
10 9 8 7 6 5 4 3 2 1

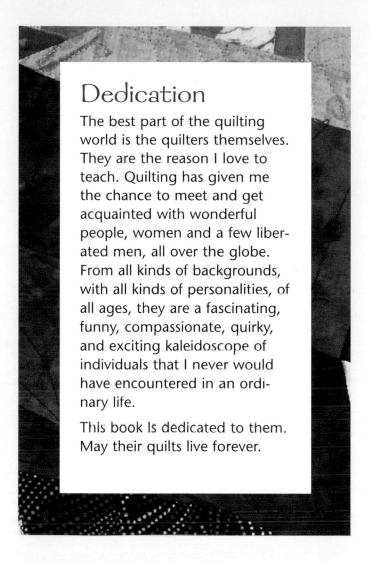

Dedication

The best part of the quilting world is the quilters themselves. They are the reason I love to teach. Quilting has given me the chance to meet and get acquainted with wonderful people, women and a few liberated men, all over the globe. From all kinds of backgrounds, with all kinds of personalities, of all ages, they are a fascinating, funny, compassionate, quirky, and exciting kaleidoscope of individuals that I never would have encountered in an ordinary life.

This book Is dedicated to them. May their quilts live forever.

Acknowledgments

I would like to thank Paulette Peters and Rhoda Cohen for the wonderful examples they kindly provided for this book. And thank you to the editors and staff of C&T, many of them quiltmakers, for their advice, enthusiasm, and technical expertise. Thank you to Jane Norberg, a friend of forty-five years, for patiently posing as a model for some of these images.

I also want to acknowledge and thank Pfaff Sewing Machines and Hobbs batting for their fine products.

Most of all, I would like to thank my students; they are the community who inspired this book.

I hope you will find the designs in this book fun to use to commemorate your love of piecing, quilting, and your quilting friends.

Introduction

I often have included human figures in my pieced art quilts. Indeed figures have often appeared in quilts, although usually as appliquéd, painted, or embroidered images. The Harriet Powers* quilts are memorable instances, Sunbonnet Sue is ever-present, and other figures appear occasionally.

I love the challenge of planning pieced quilts, figuring out how to build the images within the piecing process, and designing with available fabrics. I want my figures pieced into the quilt in the same way that the triangles and squares are pieced in traditional designs.

Use the designs to make wallhangings that surround you with color, or as bed quilts to keep you warm. The quilted sewing machines and rotary cutters will be much more comfortable to cuddle up with than their real-life counterparts.

Use the blocks as gifts for your friends, perhaps to celebrate a memorable quilt they have made, or to remember a workshop or trip you took together. Or make a quilt for the volunteers who give many hours to your guild.

Feel free to personalize the coloring and clothing, or to adapt the hairstyles or quilts-in-progress to match the recipient of your gift. Embellish to your heart's content—with scraps and trinkets sewn on the surface, or by adding a collection of guild pins and mementos.

These are quilt designs to celebrate the quilters.

Harriet Powers (1837-1911), an African-American seamstress from the Athens, Georgia area, was born into slavery. She pieced and appliquéd two wonderful quilts between 1895 and 1898. One is presently in the collection of the Museum of Fine Arts, Boston, and one is in the Smithsonian's American History Museum.

Table of Contents

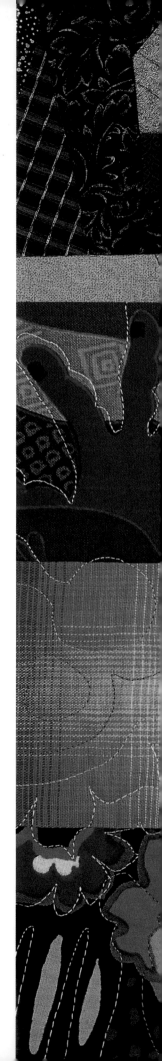

Dedication.................................3

Acknowledgments 3

Introduction 3

Getting Started...........................7

Design and Fabric........................17

The Blocks 28

    Machine Piecing   *Linda* 29

    Sewing on a Featherweight   *Nancy*.... 33

    Hand Sewing   *Karen*................. 37

    Using a Rotary Cutter   *Joan*......... 40

    Your Iron Is Your Friend   *Patty*....... 44

    And a Yard of This One   *Rose* 47

    This Is an Interesting Fabric
    Libby, Mary, and Anne 50

    Fondling Fabric   *Nina*............... 53

    Folding Up the Leftovers   *Judy*....... 57

    Choosing a Palette of Fabrics
    Dorothy and Harriet 60

    Pinning on a Design Wall   *Natalie*...... 64

    Auditioning Fabric   *Pamela*.......... 68

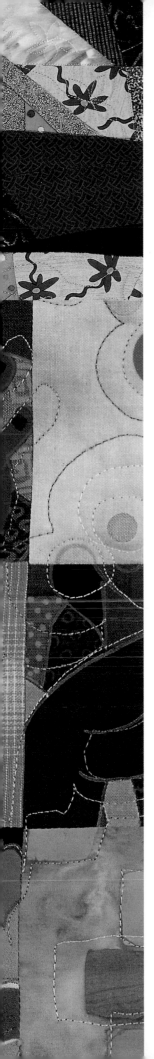

Sharing the Process
Cynthia, Vickie, and Norah 72

Design Workshop
Karen, Lucy, and Janet 76

Hand Quilting on a Big Frame   *Jane* . . . 80

Hand Quilting in a Hoop   *Chris* 83

Machine Quilting   *Kathy* 87

Repeated Block Quilts 90

Meandering 91

Whizzy Whackers 94

Spinning Featherweights 97

Small Wallhangings and Samplers 100

Small Wallhangings from Single Blocks 101

Setting a Scene 103

Using the Blocks to Make a Sampler 107

Conclusion 110

About the Author 111

Index 112

Getting Started

All of the blocks in this book are designed to be sewn with simple straight seams. They can be sewn on any sewing machine with a good straight stitch, even your grandmother's treadle machine. You sew from cut edge to cut edge—no backstitching is required. The blocks may also be pieced by hand if you prefer.

Templates

These blocks are designed to be cut and sewn using templates. Learning to use templates is well worth your while; it is much quicker than foundation piecing, and with practice, can be just as accurate. You can also control the direction in which you press the seam allowances, which makes a tremendous difference in the look of the block.

The freezer paper template method described below is very accurate. You match tic (registration) marks, then sew along the edge of the freezer paper as a guide. The freezer paper also stabilizes bias edges while you sew. Since the paper is not stitched over, like it is with paper-foundation piecing, it is much easier to remove when the piecing is finished.

This method also allows you to cut fabric and preview your block before you sew. If you see fabrics that do not work well in your design, they are easy to change.

In addition to freezer paper templates, you can make plastic templates. Your choice depends on how many blocks you intend to make and your sewing preferences. Read on to decide which method you prefer.

Degree of Difficulty

If you are new to this style of piecing, keep the following in mind when selecting a block to work on.

- ◆ A block with a few pieces is easier to sew than a block with many pieces.
- ◆ A big block with big pieces is easier to sew than a little block with little pieces.
- ◆ To make any block easier to sew, make it bigger (even much bigger) than the minimum enlargement size suggested in the text.

Block Diagrams

Each block is illustrated with a small-scale Block Diagram that has been reduced in size to fit on the book page. You will need to enlarge the Block Diagram to an appropriate size for piecing. Below each Block Diagram is an enlargement percentage suggesting the recommended minimum size for piecing the block. You may, of course, make the block larger. Bigger is always easier. Very large blocks often make dramatic wallhangings or bed quilts. Follow the procedure below to make enlargements.

Figuring the Enlargement

Many copiers can enlarge a maximum of 200%, some 400%, and some only 140%. If the copier cannot make the desired enlargement in one step, enlarge the Block Diagram as much as you can for a first step. Then enlarge the copy. You may need to do this several times.

You can figure enlargement percentages easily and accurately on a small calculator using the following method:

(Desired dimension ÷ Present dimension)
x 100
= Percentage to enlarge

To use this method, the dimensions of the block must be in decimals. Use the following table to convert fractions to decimals.

1/16"	.0625	9/16"	.5625
1/8"	.125	5/8"	.625
3/16"	.1875	11/16"	.6875
1/4"	.25	3/4"	.75
5/16"	.3125	13/16"	.8125
3/8"	.375	7/8"	.875
1/2"	.5	15/16"	.9375

As an example, 3⅞" would be entered on the calculator as 3.875. Round off numbers after you have done the calculation.

For example, if you want your block to be 14" high, and the Block Diagram is presently 5" high:

14 (inches) ÷ 5 (inches) = 2.8 x 100 = 280%

Enlarge the 5" block by 280% to get the desired 14" size.

If the copier only enlarges a maximum 200%, enlarge the 5" block by 200% to get a 10" block, then recalculate.

14 (inches) ÷ 10 (inches) = 1.4 x 100 = 140%

Enlarge the 10" block by 140% to get the desired 14" block.

This may look harder than it is. Just try it on a calculator, and you'll see how easy it is.

Making the Enlargement

After you figure out the enlargement percentage, you need to use a copier to do the enlarging. Commercial copy centers have large machines that can enlarge images up to 11" x 17" or even 17" x 22". They may also have machines that can copy onto rolls of 36"-wide paper. Copy centers that cater to architects and builders can usually make these big copies. With small copy machines, you may have to copy the block in sections, and tape them together.

Coloring the Enlarged Block Diagram

If your copy of the enlarged Block Diagram was made in black and white, you may want to use colored pencils to lightly color it to match the Block Diagram in the book. This will help you keep track of which fabrics to use for the different pieces.

Permission to Copy for Your Own Use: *The legal page in the front of this book gives you permission to make copies of the blocks for your own use. Some copy centers will ask to see this page to make sure that you have permission and are not violating standard copyright procedures.*

As with all copyrighted materials, remember that you do not have permission to make copies of these blocks for friends or for classes. Each friend or student should buy a copy of the book for their personal use.

Freezer Paper Templates

Freezer paper is a white (or tan) paper with a light plastic coating on one side that allows it to be temporarily adhered to fabric—a feature that makes it perfect to use for templates. It is readily available on rolls in most quilt shops and many grocery stores in the United States. It may be that freezer paper is used more frequently today for quilting than it is for wrapping meat.

There are many ways to use freezer paper templates in quilting. With this method, the freezer paper templates will be ironed onto the back of the selected fabrics. Although this may be a different way of using freezer paper than you have been taught, you will soon see the advantages.

Tracing the Enlarged Block Diagram

To begin the process, tape freezer paper, shiny side up, onto your enlarged Block Diagram. Trace all of the seam lines and the outside edge of the block onto the shiny side of the freezer paper. Use a ruler and a permanent marker such as an Extra or Ultra Fine Point Sharpie or Identipen permanent marker. These brands dry rapidly and will not smudge. Mark the section lines (the heavier lines) on the Block Diagram with a slightly heavier marker or a different color, if desired.

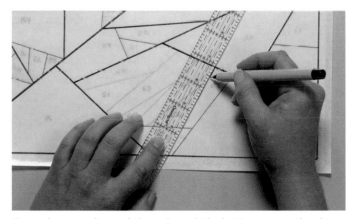

Trace the seam lines of the enlarged Block Diagram on the shiny side of freezer paper.

Tip: *If the freezer paper is too narrow for your enlarged pattern, join two pieces by butting the edges and taping them together with masking tape on the* ***dull*** *side. Masking tape is paper based and will not melt on your iron.*

Labeling the Dull Side of the Freezer Paper

Turn the freezer paper over so that the dull side is up. On the dull side, you will mark and label templates so that you can easily put the block together after it has been cut apart. The first time I tried this process, I labeled each template on the shiny side of the freezer paper to match the Block Diagram. When I ironed the templates, shiny side down on the back of the fabrics, I could no longer read the labels.

Occasionally you may find that a faint trace of ink will transfer to the back of the fabric. Let the inked freezer paper dry for a few minutes to eliminate this problem. I do not find it bothersome if a faint trace of the seam line transfers to the back of the fabric, but I don't want traces of labeling to show up in the center of a very light fabric.

Marking the Outside Edge

Use a colored pencil or highlighter to draw a line just inside the outer edges of the block. You can draw this line free-hand or use a ruler if you prefer.

This colored line will tell you what pieces form the outside edge of the block, making the block easier to reassemble after all the pieces have been cut. For ease in sewing and handling the completed blocks, put this colored edge on the straight grain of the fabric (lined up with the lengthwise or crosswise threads of the cloth) when ironing the freezer paper templates to the fabric.

Draw a line on the dull side just inside the outer edge of the block.

Marking the Section Lines

Also on the dull side of the freezer paper, use a colored pencil or highlighter to mark the section lines. The heavier lines in the Block Diagrams show the section divisions, or you can refer to the Piecing Diagrams that show the separated sections.

Trace over section lines on the dull side of freezer paper.

Labeling Each Template

Refer to the Block Diagram to mark each freezer paper template with the label that indicates its section and piecing order (A1, B7, H12, and so on). Be sure to make these labels with a **pencil** on the dull side of the freezer paper. Note that the dull side of the freezer paper is the mirror image of the Block Diagram.

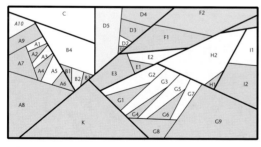

The Block Diagram

Make label on the dull side of the freezer paper.

When labeling the templates, some people can make the reversal easily, but others find it more challenging. Try these methods that some of my students use.

◆ Photocopy the small Block Diagram as a mirror image (an option on some copiers).
◆ Copy the Block Diagram onto clear acetate, turn the acetate over, and use it as a guide.
◆ Place the enlarged Block Diagram face down on a light box or window and tape the freezer paper dull side up on top, matching the seam lines.

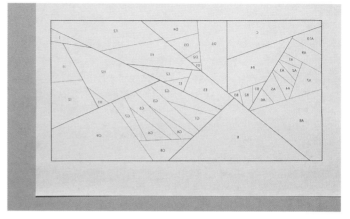

Reversed Block Diagram made by using the mirror image feature on a copier

While you are labeling each template, note (in pencil) how the pieces are used. For example, note background, hair, skin, sewing machine, and so on. Also note if you want one edge of a piece lighter or darker to create shading or shadows.

Write notes on the dull side of templates.

Tip: *If you plan to use a striped fabric, draw an arrow on the dull side of the freezer paper template in the direction you want the stripe to go.*

Making the Tic Marks

Again on the dull side of the freezer paper, draw short tic marks with a pencil across the seams at intersections and about every inch along the seams. Don't make tics closer than one inch. If you do, you are more likely to try to match the wrong tics. Some students use colored pencils for the tics, making one red, one blue, and one yellow. They find matching the colors helpful when assembling the block.

Mark tics with a pencil on the dull side.

Auditioning the Fabrics

Before you start cutting your templates and fabrics, place the actual fabrics you intend to use on a table or pin them to a design wall on top of the enlarged Block Diagram.

Any color scheme you may have envisioned before beginning a quilt, or that you may have drawn in a small-scale colored pencil sketch will need to be adjusted as you begin to work with actual fabrics.

Color works differently at actual quilt size than it does on a small mock-up. Color also works differently in fabric, especially patterned fabric, as compared to paint or colored pencils.

Add, change, or move the fabrics, making adjustments as needed. When you have a palette that pleases you at arm's length, make sure to move some distance away and look again. You want the fabrics to work well close up, as well as from across the room. Some small-scale patterns become gray or almost solids from a short distance.

Cutting the Templates

Because you drew the block on the freezer paper as a whole, when you cut the block apart, the freezer paper templates will fit back together just the way you drew them. When you sew along the edges of the freezer paper matching the tic marks, the fabric pieces will fit together as well. This is not necessarily true if you draw your block onto the freezer paper in sections, rather than as a whole block.

As you select fabrics, cut the freezer paper block apart along the seam lines using a rotary cutter and mat. If you prefer, you can use scissors to cut carefully along the lines. You may want to cut the freezer paper along the section lines as a first step; then cut the templates piece-by-piece from each section as you need them.

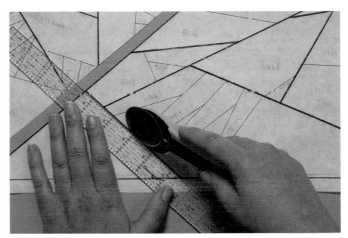

Cut freezer paper templates carefully.

Start with the fabric selections that are most critical to the design. Select and cut the skin and hair fabrics since these are the trickiest to get right. Next, cut the clothing fabrics because they must look good with the skin and hair. Feel free to give your quilter a new wardrobe. Choose clothing fabrics that set off the skin and hair choices and set off the figure well. Then choose the fabrics for the quilt or fabric your quilter is working with, and for her sewing machine if she has one. Lastly, choose the table and background fabrics to complement your previous choices.

Ironing the Freezer Paper to the Fabric

As you select fabric and cut the templates, iron each freezer paper template (shiny side down) on the back of the selected fabric. It is not necessary to pay any attention to grain line of the fabric pieces except for the pieces on the outside edges of the block (see Marking the Outside Edge on page 9). Those pieces should be placed on the straight grain of the fabric.

Iron the templates shiny side down on the back side of the fabric. Keep templates at least ½" apart.

Keep each freezer paper template at least ½" away from every other template. Each template is the finished size; you add seam allowances when cutting.

Ironing Tips: *I use a cotton setting with steam. You will have to experiment since irons are variable. You want the freezer paper to adhere firmly, yet peel off completely. If the iron is too cool, the freezer paper will fall off too soon. Rarely, and for unknown reasons, you may find a fabric that will not allow the freezer paper to be peeled off easily. Heat the fabric again quickly with the iron, and pull the paper off while it is warm. Washing all your fabrics before using them seems to eliminate this very rare problem.*

Adding Seam Allowances to the Fabric Pieces

On a cutting mat, use a clear ruler and align the ¼" line of the ruler with the edge of the freezer paper. Cut with a rotary cutter along the edge of the ruler to add perfect ¼" seam allowances.

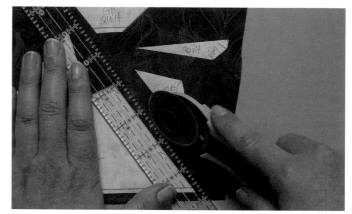

Add ¼" seam allowances to fabric pieces when cutting.

Pinning Fabric Pieces on the Block Diagram

As you cut the fabric for each piece of the block, pin each piece (with the freezer paper still on the back) in place on the enlarged Block Diagram. The seam allowances will overlap, but you will be able to see what your block will look like in actual fabric.

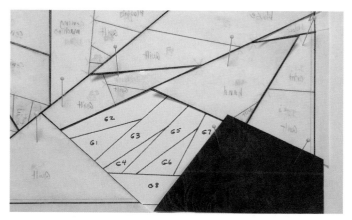

Pin each piece of fabric on the enlarged Block Diagram.

Continue cutting and pinning your fabric pieces. If you don't like the way a particular fabric looks in the block, peel off the freezer paper template, select another fabric, and try again. The freezer paper templates can be reused at least five or six times.

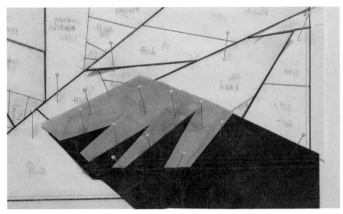

Continue pinning to preview the block; seam allowances will overlap.

The Piecing Process

The Piecing Diagram

Each Block Diagram has an accompanying Piecing Diagram. This is a picture of how the block is most easily sewn together in sections. You will sew the pieces for each section together, then sew the sections to each other as you make the block. Keep the Piecing Diagram for the block next to your sewing machine.

The Sewing Directions

The Sewing Directions describe the sewing order for each block. These directions provide the best sequence for sewing the blocks together. Follow them carefully for the best results.

Sewing Tip: *If you like, you can chain piece many of these pairs of pieces. To chain piece, sew a pair. Stop the machine and line up the next pair of pieces. Start the machine, feeding in the next pair. Repeat this process. When several have been sewn, clip the sewn pairs apart.*

Sewing the Blocks

Match edges and tic marks carefully using fine silk pins (.5 mm). The pins commonly sold as "quilting" pins are too big and will distort the fabric, preventing you from sewing accurate seams.

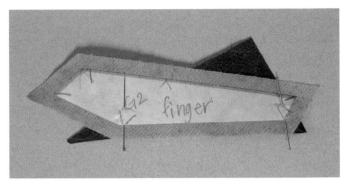

Match tics and edges of the templates. Pin.

Sew along the edge of the freezer paper. Start the seam at the cut edge and sew all the way across to the opposite cut edge. I use a stitch length of 2.0 mm or 12 stitches to the inch.

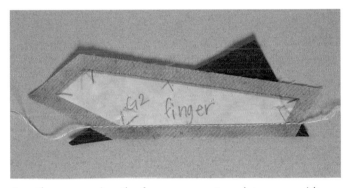

Sew the seam using the freezer paper template as a guide.

Don't remove the freezer paper until the entire block is sewn together. The paper stabilizes all the bias edges and makes the sewing easier and more accurate.

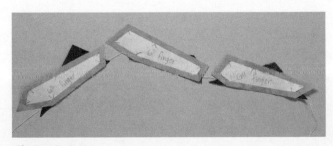

Chain piecing

Pressing Seam Allowances

As you sew, press the seam allowances in the direction of the small arrows on the Piecing Diagram. I use a steam iron. The seam allowances will pad the edge of one piece and give the surface a little dimension. Ignore traditional quilt pressing rules.

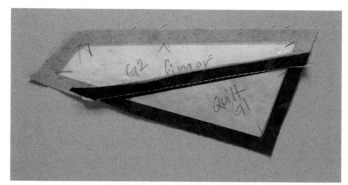

Press seam allowances in direction of the arrows on the Piecing Diagram.

Repeated Blocks

I love traditional block quilts, especially the overall patterns formed by the repeated blocks. As a connection to this quilting style, three quilts in this book were made from repeated blocks. These repeated blocks were adapted to simplify and intensify the graphic quality of selected portions of several blocks. See *Meandering* on page 91, *Whizzy Whackers* on page 94, and *Spinning Featherweights* on page 97.

Several options for making templates for these repeated blocks are described below.

Freezer Paper Templates for Repeated Blocks

You can make up to four copies of a freezer paper block at one time. Stack four pieces of freezer paper shiny side up, or dull side up if you want any blocks to be reversed. Put your traced block on top. Staple or pin the layers together.

Remove the top thread from your sewing machine. With an old needle and a short stitch length, sew through all layers following the lines on your traced block. This will perforate each layer of paper with your block pattern. Use each freezer paper copy as you would a traced block.

Making Mirror Images: *Keep in mind that when making a mirror or reversed block you will make left-handed quilters and left-handed sewing machines. While I know many delightful left-handed quilters, left-handed sewing machines are rare indeed.*

Plastic Templates for Repeated Blocks

Another method of making templates for a repeated block is to use template plastic. Start with a paper copy of your block at the size you want to sew. Label the pieces in the block according to the Piecing Diagram. Mark tics at intersections and about 1" apart along seam lines. (Remember—don't make tics closer than 1" as it is then more likely that you may try to match the wrong tics.) Cut the paper block apart. Glue or tape each paper piece to template plastic. Remember to leave at least ½" between templates. Cut out each plastic template with a ¼" seam allowance added beyond the edge of the paper. With a ⅛" hole punch (available at some fabric and craft stores), punch a small hole at each tic and corner.

A stack of fabrics can be cut with these plastic templates. Layer four to eight fabrics back side up. Iron the stack with a steam iron. Put the plastic template on top, wrong side up. Either trace the template with a pencil, then cut the stack with very sharp scissors, or cut very carefully using a ruler and rotary cutter.

For accurate sewing, mark a small pencil dot through the punched holes on the back side of each fabric piece. Match and pin the dots together as needed before sewing each seam.

Design and Fabric

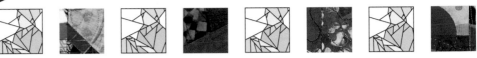

In this book, I have given you many pieced block designs of quiltmakers doing quilterly things. Some are sewing by hand, some designing, some sewing by machine, some enjoying a friendly conversation. These blocks are ready to enlarge and use.

For those of you interested in the design process of these blocks, or for those interested in designing your own blocks, the beginning of this chapter will explain a little about how these blocks came to be.

Designing Figures for Piecing

Translating a three-dimensional figure into a pieced block of straight seams can be a tricky challenge. The figure must be greatly simplified, but still "read" well. I usually begin the design by working from a careful freehand drawing or a line tracing from a photograph.

On a piece of tracing paper placed over the initial drawing, I begin to change the drawing to a series of straight lines, working simultaneously with the outline of the figure and the interior shapes. Very slight shifts in angle or choice of direction can make a tremendous difference in outcome. See my book *Piecing: Expanding the Basics,* especially pages 92–144, for a detailed discussion of the process.

While tracing and adjusting, I am very aware of the sewing process. To make the sewing easier, I plan the sections carefully so they come apart cleanly. Limiting the sewing to straight seams forces an additional degree of abstraction in the figure drawing that I enjoy.

Original Natalie   **Revised** *Natalie*

Design Challenge #1: Too Many Pieces

In making a drawing of Natalie stretching up to pin a piece on her design wall, I loved all the folds and wrinkles in her clothing. I planned my first Natalie to include many of them.

However, the block used a great number of pieces and seemed more complicated than it needed to be. The area around Natalie's chin and shoulder included a number of very small pieces that were fussy and easy to lose in the sewing process.

Starting over, I drew a new pattern for Natalie that works just as well as an image, but is much easier to sew. I eliminated some of the folds and wrinkles in her clothing, and changed the angle of her head slightly.

Design Challenge #2: Shaping the Figure

In my first pattern for *Choosing a Palette of Fabrics,* the figures of Dorothy and Harriet were awkward. While the outline of Dorothy (on the left) was okay, the seaming inside the figure looked arbitrary. It didn't relate to Dorothy's anatomy well enough, although some of the problem was with the choice of the pink plaid fabric for her dress. In addition, Dorothy's arms and hands were

too crude, and Harriet's head did not connect to her body. Her jaw line was too square, and her right hand was awkwardly drawn.

In the revised block, I've changed the seaming in Dorothy, dressed her in a short-sleeved blouse and jumper, and redrawn her arms and left hand. She works much better as a figure now. I also changed the piecing of Harriet's head and hand to correct some of the faults in my first attempt.

Drawing figures for piecing is always a careful balancing act. In this case, the new block has more pieces than the first version. Compare the two blocks and see if you think the additional piecing is worth it for the sake of the resulting image.

Original Dorothy and Harriet

Revised *Dorothy and Harriet*

Original Joan

Revised *Joan*

Design Challenge #3: Finding the Focus

My original plan for the *Rotary Cutting* block showed the whole figure of Joan perched on her sewing chair with her sneakered feet on tiptoe as she digs in with her rotary cutter.

Although I liked the pose and the way the sneakers and the base of the chair came out, they were distracting from the action of the rotary cutter. The image needed to be cropped.

Compare the new rotary block with the old one. I've intensified the focus by cropping, and the new block now focuses on the process I intended to illustrate. I've also changed Joan's hairstyle. It was very short and close to her head in the first block, and I've redrawn her hair in a looser style to fly around with the speed of her motion with the rotary cutter.

See *Whizzy Whackers* on page 94 for further cropping of this block to make a simpler graphic image for use as a repeated block.

Experimenting with Cropping:

When working from a photograph or a drawing, you can experiment with the cropping process by cutting two L-shaped pieces of heavy white paper. Use them to frame different parts of an image before settling on what to select for your design.

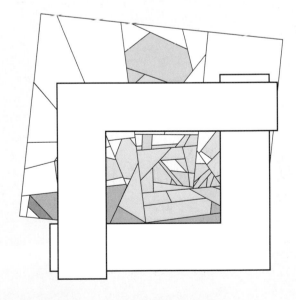

Experiment with cropped images.

Original Linda   **Revised** *Linda*

Design Challenge #4: Refining the Figure

In my first attempt at *Machine Piecing* with Linda at her sewing machine, I had some problems both with fabric choices and the pieced image.

The fabric I chose for Linda's blouse was a strong medium scale print. I hoped the breaks in the printed pattern from one piece of the blouse to the next would be enough so that the sleeve would be seen as separate from the bodice, but the print flowed together when the block was sewn. I also wanted to redesign Linda's hair and left hand.

For the new Linda block, I used three different fabrics for her blouse: a stripe for the sleeves, a patchwork design for the blouse yoke, and a darker print for the bodice. These fabrics define the figure much better. This same approach to clothing is used in several other blocks in this book as well (see *Using a Rotary Cutter* on page 40, *This is an Interesting Fabric* on page 50, and *Folding Up the Leftovers* on page 57).

I also loosened up Linda's hairdo and redrew the left hand that guides her sewing, adding a separate little finger and a seam across the knuckles.

You will find that designing for machine piecing requires many compromises and some very subtle adjustments to produce good results. I aim to make the figures as simple as possible to sew, but at the same time, I also try to give them a lot of character. The blocks in this book are the result of a lot of practice. It's fun to do, but challenging to figure out. If the process intrigues you, I urge you to design some of your own.

Choosing Fabrics

Quilters have often complimented me on my use of unusual printed fabrics, especially in my art quilts. I must confess I have a lot of fun finding interesting prints in the first place, then pulling them out of my stash, maybe years later, and combining them in a quilt composition. Fellow quilters Nancy Halpern and Rhoda Cohen started me on this path in 1978. Along with quilter Sylvia Einstein, we have egged each other on ever since, seeing who could find and use the most unique prints. Each of us uses printed fabrics in her own individual way.

An important part of my quilting style is my deliberate use of fabrics that make a clear statement that this is a **quilt**, not a painting or photograph, or even a naturalistic representation of a subject. I use commercially available fabrics in an impressionistic way rather than drawing, painting, or embroidering literal details. Personally, I resist using fabrics with printed images that represent clouds in the sky or trees on a hill in very literal ways. I much prefer to imply the clouds or trees with other types of prints. If someone gives me photographically literal cloud fabric, I'll most likely use it for my grandmother's gray hair, or maybe a sheep. I don't want the fabric manufacturer to be the designer of the quilt. I'm in charge of that part of the process.

If you are interested in learning to use unusual prints, you don't need to invest a lot of money. Get fat quarters or explore samples, seconds, rummage sales, clothing scraps, or thrift shops. I tell my students "If you don't have it, you'll never learn to use it." But, like any learning process, it will take time and effort on your part.

Fabrics that Cut Up Well

When looking for fabrics to use, especially for this type of piecework, try to find fabrics that will look slightly different in each cut piece. This can be a challenge because many printed fabrics for quiltmakers are uniform patterns, designed by the manufacturers so each cut piece looks, more or less, like every other piece. For example, if the fabric is a polka dot, the polka dots are usually almost evenly spaced. I find polka-dot fabrics much more interesting to use in quilts if the dots are randomly arranged so that some cut pieces have one dot, or a sprinkling of three, or a tight cluster and a couple of single dots, or even no dots at all!

The yellow polka-dot fabric below, one of several colorways from Alexander Henry, meets my test for a truly useful fabric for quilts. The fabric has a great variety of sizes of dots, a random spacing that I love, and some transparency effects where the dots overlap. When cut into pieces, 3" to 6" squares and triangles for example, each cut piece has a unique printed design.

In addition to randomly cutting this fabric, I exploited the large red-orange dots in the little quilt in *Hand Quilting on a Big Frame* (see page 80).

Two other useful fabrics, also from Alexander Henry, are related large-scale prints. I did not choose them because of the Japanese figures; in fact, I would have preferred them to be less ethnically specific. I like these fabrics for the hand imagery and the wonderful variety of pieces they produce when cut up into patchwork-sized pieces. Even randomly cut, each square or triangle of the fabric contains a different graphic pattern. Each square or triangle almost looks like it is itself a piece of patchwork (see the triangles in the border of *Machine Quilting Wallhanging* on page 101).

The multicolored hands on both fabrics could be holding needles. Whether that was the fabric designer's intention or not, I don't know. I fussy cut some squares to use in the sashing of the *Sampler Quilt* shown on page 106.

Yellow polka-dot fabric

Two large-scale "Japanese" prints

Preview Print Fabrics: *Explore the possibilities in print fabrics by cutting a square or triangular opening the size of your desired quilt piece in a piece of white paper. Slide this window around the fabric and notice the designs that appear in the hole.*

You can center an image and fussy cut. But an image may be more intriguing if part of the original design is obscured.

Choosing Fabrics for Skin

I prefer to use patterned fabrics such as prints, plaids, or batiks for skin. The patterns on the fabrics can suggest facial features in a subtle way, and can be fussy cut to differentiate areas of skin using the shading within the fabric or changing angles of grain or pattern. Most solid colored fabrics read too flat. I like to use calicos or prints for skin, even though they may contain leaves, flowers, or curlicues.

Some good fabrics for skin

When piecing human figures, I often select poses in which the face is somewhat obscured, rather than full face. This is true for most of the figures in this book. But the poses were also selected because the intent was to focus on the figures making quilts, or interacting with others in that process, rather than making a portrait of an individual.

I realize that the selection of skin fabrics can be a political minefield. The best I can do as a teacher and artist is to tell you what I think about the subject. You will have to make your own choices for your own quilts.

As a teacher, I often wish that I could delete color names. The mentality of thinking "the sky is blue," "the grass is green," "tree trunks are brown," keeps people from actually learning to look, and from using their eyes to see.

When choosing skin color for your figures, forget the words *white, black, red,* and *yellow.* Literal **white** fabric makes your figure look like a ghost. Literal **black** fabric is not nearly as effective in giving your figure life as very deep values of other hues.

Skin color is tremendously variable on an individual; the palms of the hands are lighter than the backs of the hands for instance. The play of light on a figure is also important in making your figure look persuasive. Look carefully at where you want the light and shadow to fall on your figure.

You will probably find that really good skin selection is trickier than it might appear: a little too red may look sunburned, a little too yellow like a case of jaundice, and a little too green like a fatal illness.

You can, of course, make the skin bright red or blue or purple if you wish, and opt out of any naturalistic issues. See the printed hands in the Alexander Henry prints on page 21.

With some figures, I chose a skin print that is a uniform pattern, as with Patty in *Your Iron Is Your Friend.*

Patty

With other figures, I chose a print with more variety, and fussy cut the pieces to shape the edges, as in Jane's hand, shown in *Handquilting on a Big Frame*.

You may find you need to incorporate different skin fabrics in a single figure, using one for the face and a different one for a neck, to keep these two areas from blending together, as I did with Mary in *This Is an Interesting Fabric*. You can also differentiate these areas with different quilting patterns or thread colors.

Jane

Mary

Using Floral Fabric For Skin:

I used a floral fabric for Judy's face. The print on the fabric implies facial details without being literal. Actually the curlicue looks kind of like a nose, but I think that may be due to serendipity rather than something I actually planned.

Judy

Choosing Fabrics for Hair

You'll see a variety of hair fabrics in these blocks as well. Some are almost literal hair prints such as Karen. Others are fussy cut from brown leaves, such as Chris and Kathy. Jane's gray hair is cut from a feather print. In most cases, I have loosely machine quilted the hair with variegated threads, running the quilting lines past the seam edges of the pieced hair to soften and loosen it up.

Kathy

Karen

Jane

Chris

Relative Values in Fabrics

Interacting with all of these fabric choice considerations is the challenge of making your quilt work well as a color composition and to read as you intend it to. Relative values (lightness or darkness) of adjacent fabric pieces are important to keep in mind when constructing all of the figures in this book. Because the whole block is composed of separate pieces of cloth, it is important that the pieces in the figure hold together visually. A very light blouse may blend with a light background, leaving a disembodied head and arms.

Take a careful look at the edges of figures. Using a light skin next to a light background piece may make the skin appear to be part of the background rather than part of the figure. A dark skin value next to a dark shirt may confuse the eye, blending the shirt and the figure into an undifferentiated area of color.

When selecting fabrics for adjacent parts of the block, it is more important to consider value than the hue, or color. Rather than using a navy blue shirt on a dark-skinned figure, try a lighter blue, or a blue print with a lighter pattern, to visually separate the two elements. It is usually not sufficient just to have a shirt or blouse be a different hue (color) or a different printed pattern than the background—the values, at least at the edges of the pieces, need to separate the two elements.

The handle of the iron in *Your Iron is Your Friend* shows up well against the darker fabric of Patty's shirt, but the value of the handle is the same as the value of the background pieces behind Patty. The front edge of the iron nearly blends into the wall.

I've almost saved the iron by inserting a dark piece of blouse along part of the edge. It would have been better to have used a slightly darker value for the handle, perhaps light blue or gray. This would make it stand apart from the background and still show up against her dark blouse. Alternatively, I could have moved her hand with the iron to the left so the iron was completely surrounded by blouse.

With Rhoda Cohen's *Fondling Fabric* block, you can see another example of values being too similar. Rhoda's background fabric is a shaded pink/yellow/green/blue print. Rhoda has carefully cut this fabric to place the bluer areas next to Nina's face, neck, and left arm. Notice how these parts of the figure show up more clearly than the lower edge of Nina's right arm that is the same *value* as the adjacent yellow area of the background fabric.

Detail of iron from Your Iron Is Your Friend

Detail of Fondling Fabric, *pieced by Rhoda Cohen*

Choosing Fabrics for Quilts-in-Progress

In many of the blocks in this book, the figures are working on a little quilt-in-progress. To maintain a consistent look, I've chosen bright, clear colors, high contrast, and strong geometry for my little quilts-to-be. You can personalize your blocks by making your quilts-in-progress in other styles, fabrics, and colors.

Cheater Fabrics

I'm always on the lookout for fabrics where the print looks like a little piece of patchwork, almost a miniature version of cheater fabrics in which the fabric is printed to look like a patchwork quilt.

Plaids and Checks

Some plaid or checked fabrics look like patchwork and may be a good possibility for little quilts.

Detail of quilt from Hand Quilting in a Hoop

Miniature Patchwork

If you can't find commercially printed small-scale cheater fabrics, stitch a bit of Seminole or other patchwork in the colors of your choice and cut this patchwork up for the pieces in your block. For *Hand Quilting on a Big Frame,* I fussy cut squares with red quarter circles (polka dots) from the yellow polka-dot fabric described on page 21, and pieced a miniature Mill Wheel top.

Detail of Quilt from Hand Quilting on a Big Frame

Scanned Fabric

If you have access to a computer and scanner, you can scan a photo of a quilt, print it out on fabric, and include pieces of that in your block. Wouldn't it be fun to make a small wallhanging for a friend with a scanned and printed image of one of her quilts in the block?

Left Over Blocks

Another possibility is to use a block, or portion of a block left over from another project, as source material for a quilt-in-progress. Place a block in the quilting frame of *Hand Quilting on a Big Frame* or cut up an old block for the little quilt shown in *Hand Quilting in a Hoop.*

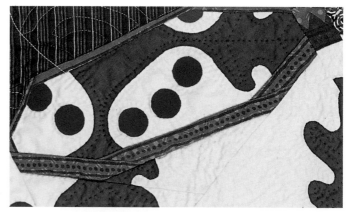

Detail of Hand Quilting in a Hoop: Oak Leaf and Cherries

You can also use these left over blocks to add an interesting and personal touch to many of the blocks. Place them under the sewing machine in *Machine Piecing, Sewing on a Featherweight,* or *Machine Quilting.* Place block on top of the ironing board in *Your Iron Is Your Friend* or on the design wall in *Pinning on a Design Wall* and *Auditioning Fabric.*

Adding Pieces to the Quilted Surface

I love the confusion of color from the scraps and piles of fabric that accumulate while I'm making a quilt. I wanted to include some of that liveliness in these blocks, but as additions to the surface, rather than as part of the piecing. That way they could be more spontaneous and loose than the carefully planned and pieced figures and sewing machines.

With the *Machine Piecing* block, I inserted a string of pieced triangles under the hand Linda is using to guide her sewing. Simply attach the triangles to the block or to the quilted quilt with a row of stitching. You can also fuse the triangles to the pieced or quilted block.

Fabrics added to a quilted block

Triangles added to a quilted block

Fusing to Prevent Fraying

Because my *Sampler Quilt* will be subject to a lot of traveling and handling, I was concerned that the edges of the triangles and other added pieces might fray. To minimize the fraying, I fused two pieces of fabric together. To make the fused fabric look like one piece of fabric, I ironed fusible web to the **wrong** side of the top piece of fabric. I then fused the top fabric to the **right** side of a second piece of fabric. The fused sandwich looks like one piece of fabric with a right side and a wrong side.

The edges of the pieces cut from this fused sandwich are raw, but the hidden fusible web prevents them from fraying. You will see this and similar techniques used in blocks throughout the book.

Fabrics added to a quilted block

The Blocks

Machine Piecing

Quilters develop a special relationship with their sewing machines. We are apt to become twitchy and extremely irritable when our favorite machines are in for repair or cleaning. That we may own another machine in addition to the missing one is barely adequate comfort. I myself own six or seven machines of historic or sentimental value in addition to the one I actually use.

At a recent workshop, the discussion of sewing machines was especially lively, and it struck me that this level of passion was perhaps incomprehensible to most of the rest of the world. The comparison that came most readily to mind was the intensity of interest with which some guys discuss their cars or their favorite sports team.

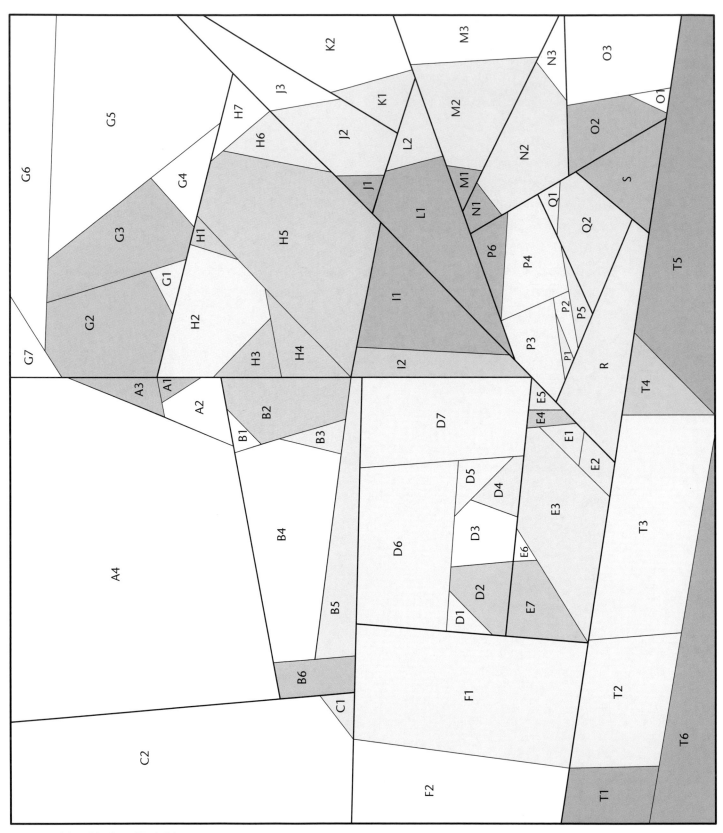

Machine Piecing *Block Diagram*

Enlarge this block 190% to a 16" x 14" rectangle, see page 8. The size suggested is the minimum practical size. To make it easier, make it bigger.

During construction, press the seam allowances in the direction indicated by the arrows on the Piecing Diagram.

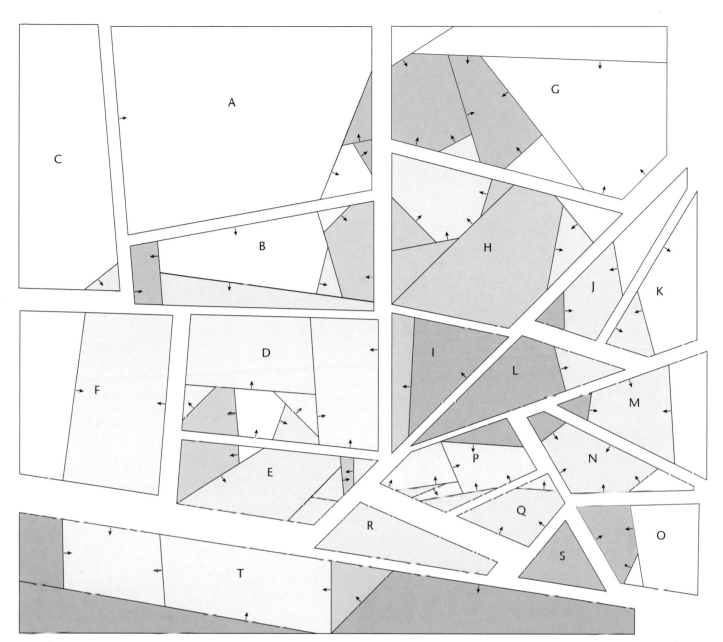

Machine Piecing *Piecing Diagram*

Sew:
A1 to A2 to A3 to A4
B1 to B2
B3 to B4 to B(1,2) to B5 to B6 to A
C1 to C2 to AB
D1 to D2 to D3 to D4 to D5 to D6 to D7
E1 to E2 to E3 to E4 to E5
E6 to E7 to E(1,2,3,4,5) to D
F1 to F2 to DE to ABC
G1 to G2
G3 to G4 to G(1,2) to G5 to G6 to G7
H1 to H2 to H3 to H4 to H5 to H6 to H7 to G

I1 to I2 to GH to ABCDEF
J1 to J2 to J3
K1 to K2 to J
L1 to L2 to JK
M1 to M2 to M3
N1 to N2 to N3 to M
O1 to O2 to O3 to MN
P1 to P2 to P3 to P4 to P5 to P6
Q1 to Q2 to P to R to S to MNO to JKL to
 ABCDEFGHI
T1 to T2 to T3 to T4 to T5 to T6 to
 ABCDEFGHIJKLMNOPQRS

Machine Piecing *with added triangles*

Linda is piecing on a generic, contemporary machine. Feel free to personalize the machine in your quilt with embroidered, sketched, or quilted details to make it your own.

I have added a string of pieced triangles to the surface of the quilted block to represent Linda's piecing. See Adding Pieces to the Quilted Surface on page 27.

Sewing on a Featherweight Nancy

Little black Singer Featherweights are a favorite sewing machine for quiltmakers to bring to workshops. In addition to sewing a good straight stitch, they seem to last forever. Their light weight makes them very easy to carry, but I think that most quilters who bring their Featherweights to class rather than a heavier machine, more than make up for the weight by bringing more *fabric!*

I have heard that you can run a Featherweight off two solar panels next to a trout stream if marital duties require you to be away from a source of electricity for awhile.

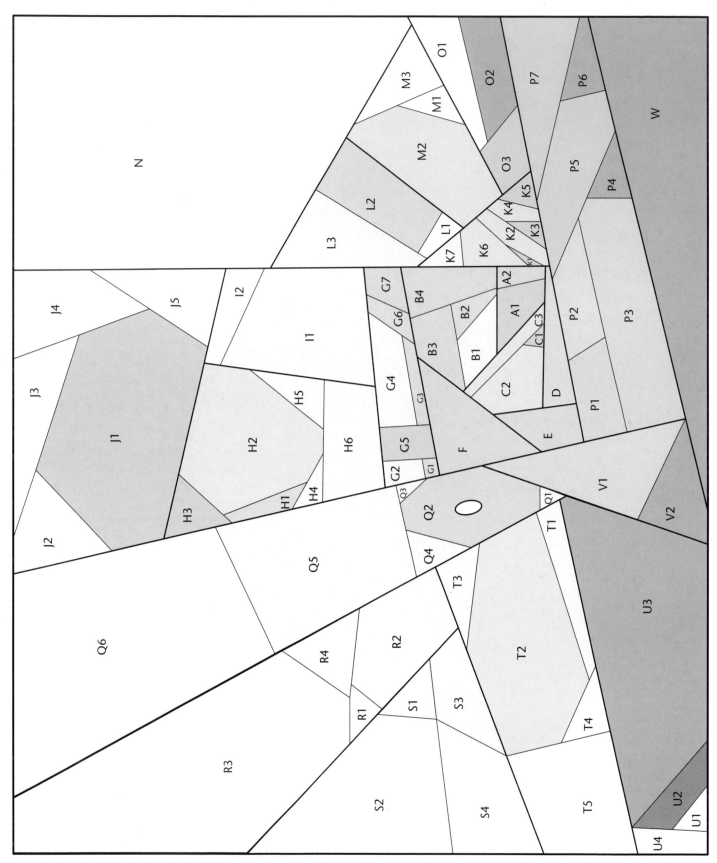

Sewing on a Featherweight *Block Diagram*

Enlarge this block 194% to a 17" x 14" rectangle, see page 8. The size suggested is the minimum practical size. To make it easier, make it bigger.

During construction, press the seam allowances in the direction indicated by the arrows on the Piecing Diagram.

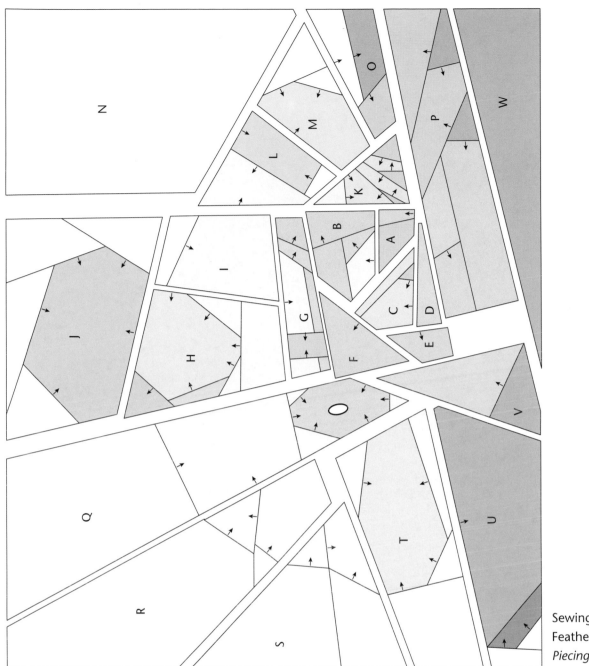

Sewing on a
Featherweight
Piecing Diagram

Sew:

A1 to A2, B1 to B2 to B3 to B4 to A

C1 to C2 to C3 to AB to D to E to F

G1 to G2 to G5

G3 to G4 to G6 to G7 to G(1,2,5) to ABCDEF

H1 to H2 to H3 to H4 to H5 to H6

I1 to I2 to H to ABCDEFG

J1 to J2 to J3 to J4 to J5 to ABCDEFGHI

K1 to K2, K3 to K4 to K5 to K(1,2) to K6 to K7

L1 to L2 to L3

M1 to M2 to M3 to L to N

O1 to O2 to O3 to LMN to K to ABCDEFGHIJ

P1 to P2 to P3 to P4 to P5 to P6 to P7 to
ABCDEFGHIJKLMNO

Q1 to Q2 to Q3 to Q4 to Q5 to Q6

R1 to R2

R3 to R4 to R(1,2)

S1 to S2

S3 to S4 to S(1,2) to R

T1 to T2 to T3 to T4 to T5 to RS

U1 to U2 to U3 to U4 to RST to Q

V1 to V2 to QRSTU to ABCDEFGHIJKLMNOP to W

Sewing on a Featherweight, *pieced by Rhoda Cohen*

Use several different black fabrics for the Featherweight to show off the different surfaces. Maybe you can find one with fine-line gold decorations to use on the machine's arm and head. To make the silver knob on the handwheel, appliqué, fuse, or quilt an oval. Or sew on a button after you've finished the quilting.

See Adding Pieces to the Quilted Surface on page 27 to embellish the surface of Nancy's table with scissors, seam ripper, spools, or a coffee cup. Maybe you can find a novelty fabric with a print of sewing items that you could use. Embroider pins with big stitches of a heavy thread and add French knots or beads for the heads.

Here's another version of this block, pieced by Rhoda Cohen. Rhoda modified Nancy's hairstyle slightly for a more contemporary look. I especially like the fabrics in the sewing machine and the fabrics in Nancy's arms, fussy cut to be shaded appropriately.

To make Nancy's left hand more dramatic and add a suggestion of a shadow, use a darker shade for the cloth she's sewing in pieces K1, K3, and K5.

Hand Sewing

Hand piecing, hand appliqué, and even stitching down a binding are relaxing, repetitive processes, creating a time to appreciate the combinations of colors and patterns, and the tactile qualities of fabric and thread. I find hand sewing a lovely contrast to using the sewing machine.

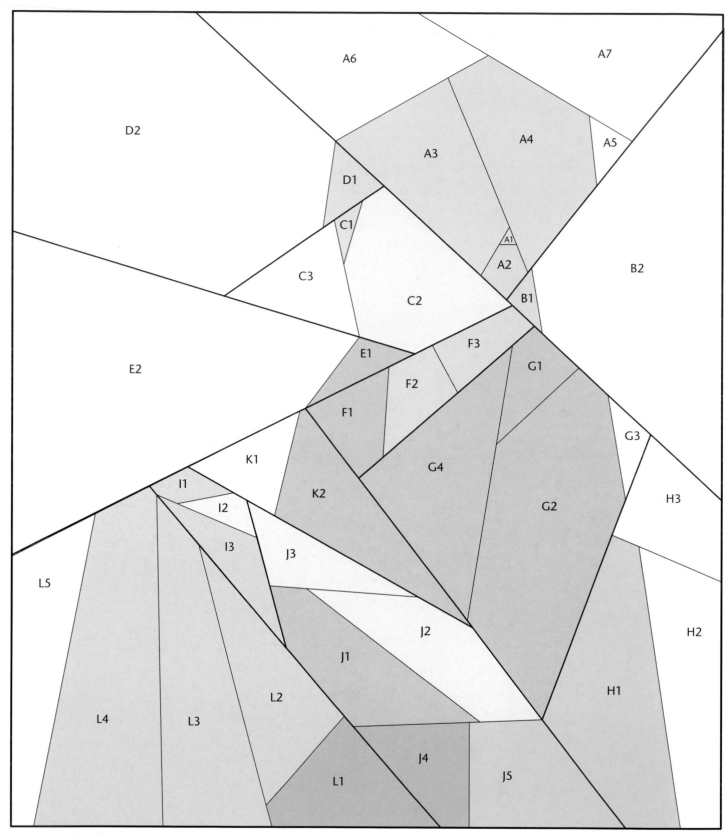

Hand Sewing *Block Diagram*

Enlarge this block 176% to a 13" x 15" rectangle, see page 8. The size suggested is the minimum practical size. To make it easier, make it bigger.

During construction, press the seam allowances in the direction indicated by the arrows on the Piecing Diagram.

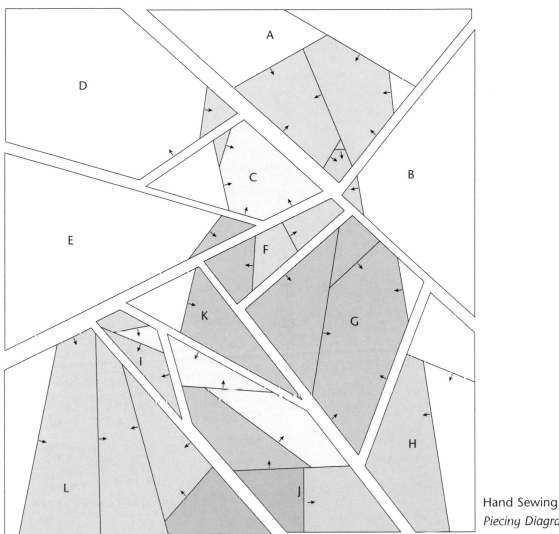

Hand Sewing
Piecing Diagram

Sew:
A1 to A2 to A3 to A4 to A5 to A6 to A7
B1 to B2 to A
C1 to C2 to C3
D1 to D2 to C
E1 to E2 to CD
F1 to F2 to F3

G1 to G2 to G3 to G4 to F
H1 to H2 to H3 to FG
I1 to I2 to I3
J1 to J2 to J3, J4 to J5 to J(1,2,3) to I
K1 to K2 to IJ
L1 to L2 to L3 to L4 to L5 to IJK to FGH to CDE
   to AB

For the pieced quilt top in Karen's hands, notice how one large-scale print, cut randomly and then pieced together, looks like patchwork. You can also use a cheater fabric here, or cut up a block left over from another project. See Choosing Fabrics for Quilts-in-Progress on page 26.

The blue plaid behind Karen's elbow may be a jacket hanging over the back of her chair, or it could be the fabric she's considering for the back of her quilt. My sewing room becomes a truly colorful place when I'm in the middle of a quilt, with fabrics that are under consideration draped or stacked or thrown on all available surfaces.

Note that I've angled the stripe of Karen's shirt in the direction of the grain line of an actual shirt and used a literal hair fabric for her hair. Notice also that the fabric for her neck and throat are slightly darker than the fabrics I used for her face. This provides enough differentiation in the skin area to separate her jaw line from her neck.

Using a Rotary Cutter Joan

For many quiltmakers, rotary cutters have replaced scissors as the tool of choice when cutting fabrics. Rotary cutters are especially useful for cutting multiple layers of fabrics accurately. Quiltmakers can whiz through the process of cutting out a quilt, a process that used to be extremely time-consuming when using cardboard templates, tracing around each one, and cutting each piece with scissors.

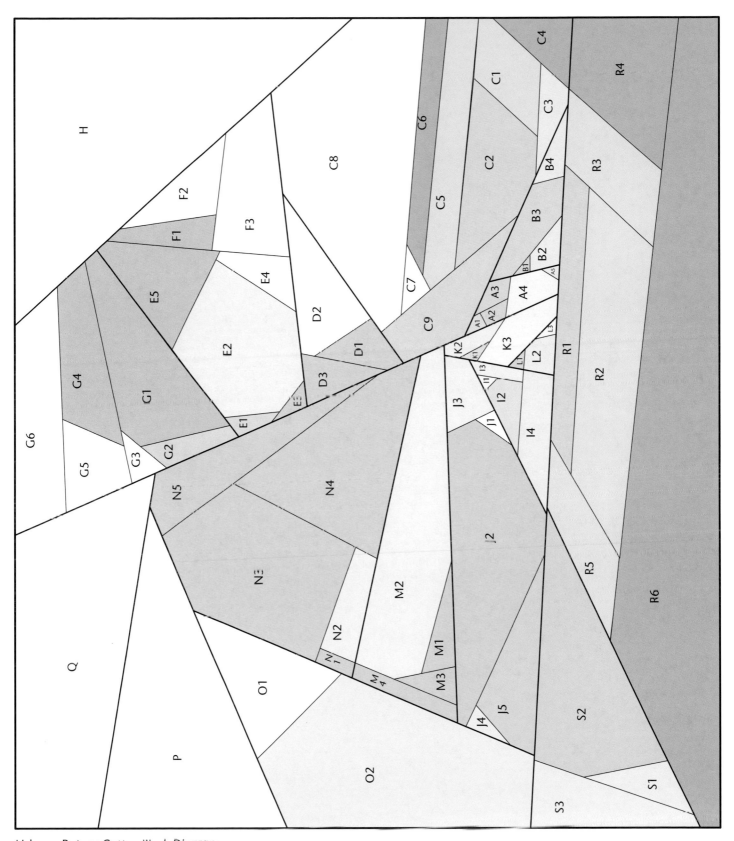

Using a Rotary Cutter *Block Diagram*

Enlarge this block 177% to a 15" x 13" rectangle, see page 8. The size suggested is the minimum practical size. To make it easier, make it bigger.

During construction, press the seam allowances in the direction indicated by the arrows on the Piecing Diagram.

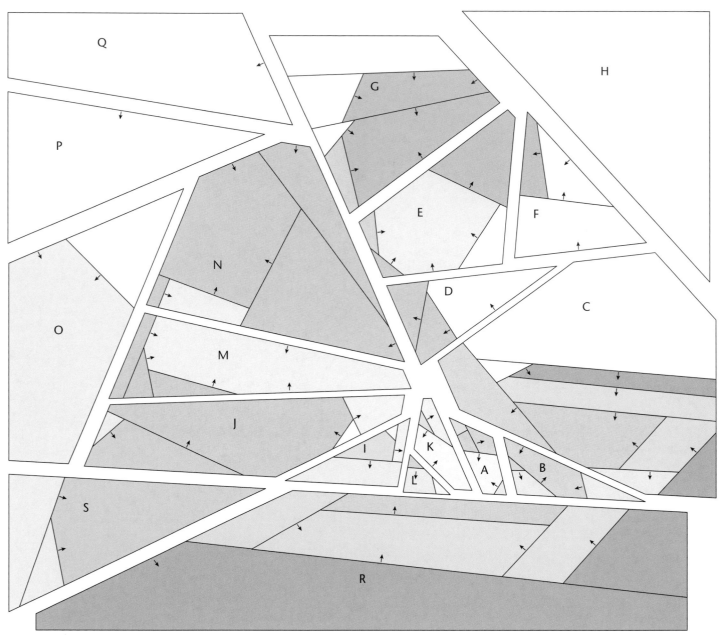

Using a Rotary Cutter *Piecing Diagram*

Sew:
A1 to A2 to A3 to A4 to A5
B1 to B2 to B3 to B4 to A
C1 to C2 to C3 to C4 to C5 to C6 to C7 to C8 to
   C9 to AB
D1 to D2 to D3 to ABC
E1 to E2 to E3 to E4 to E5
F1 to F2 to F3 to E, G1 to G2 to G3
G4 to G5 to G6 to G(1,2,3) to EF to ABCD to H

I1 to I2 to I3 to I4
J1 to J2 to J3
J4 to J5 to J(1,2,3) to I, K1 to K2 to K3
L1 to L2 to L3 to K to IJ, M1 to M2 to M3 to M4 to
   IJKL, N1 to N2 to N3 to N4 to N5 to IJKLM
O1 to O2 to IJKLMN to P to Q to ABCDEFGH
S1 to S2 to S3
R1 to R2 to R3 to R4 to R5 to R6 to S to
   ABCDEFGHIJKLMNOPQ

Using a Rotary Cutter *with added strips of fabric*

I fussy cut a yellow fabric for the rotary cutter, positioning a stylized flower where the knob should be. You can also use a plain fabric and add the knob by sewing on a button after the quilting is complete. Or you can fuse or appliqué a knob from a different fabric. See *Whizzy Whackers* on page 94.

I cut Joan's ruler from a striped fabric. I like the slight mismatch of the stripes from piece to piece because it shows how the block is put together. You can also use a plain fabric for the ruler, and quilt the ruler lines or draw them with ink.

When selecting skin fabric for Joan, choose a slightly darker value for her left arm and hand (pieces A3, B1, B3, and C9) to visually separate her left arm from her right hand. Use a darker value for her neck (pieces E1, G2) than you use for her face (piece E2), so her jaw line is visible.

To show how speedy Joan is at rotary cutting, I added extra cut strips to the quilted block. See Adding Pieces to the Quilted Surface on page 27.

Your Iron Is Your Friend

I think the invention of the electric iron was a greater boon to quilters than the electric sewing machine. In my teenage years, I used to sew Vogue Designer patterns on my grandmother's treadle machine, which worked fine once I'd mastered the rhythm. In fact, it was kind of fun. Flatirons, heated on a wood stove, are *not* fun.

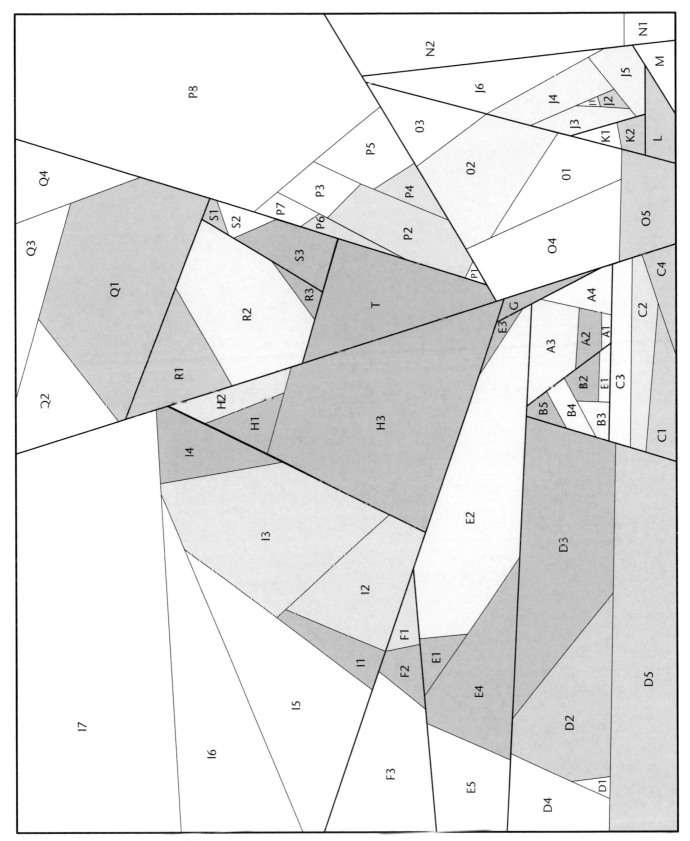

Your Iron Is Your Friend *Block Diagram*

Enlarge this block 210% to an 18" x 14½" rectangle, see page 8. The size suggested is the minimum practical size. To make it easier, make it bigger.

During construction, press the seam allowances in the direction indicated by the arrows on the Piecing Diagram.

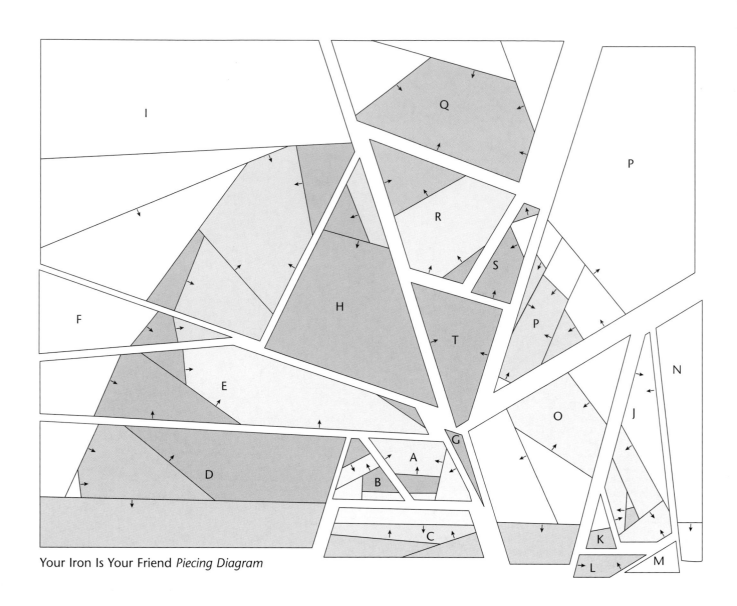

Your Iron Is Your Friend *Piecing Diagram*

Sew:
A1 to A2 to A3 to A4
B1 to B2 to B3 to B4 to B5 to A
C1 to C2 to C3 to C4 to AB
D1 to D2 to D3 to D4 to D5 to ABC
E1 to E2 to E3 to E4 to E5
F1 to F2 to F3 to E to ABCD to G
H1 to H2 to H3
I1 to I2 to I3 to I4 to I5 to I6 to I7 to H to
  ABCDEFG
J1 to J2 to J3 to J4 to J5 to J6

K1 to K2 to J to L to M
N1 to N2 to JKLM
O1 to O2 to O3 to O4 to O5 to JKLMN
P1 to P2 to P3
P4 to P5 to P(1,2,3)
P6 to P7 to P(1,2,3,4,5) to P8
Q1 to Q2 to Q3 to Q4
R1 to R2 to R3
S1 to S2 to S3 to R to Q to T to P to JKLMNO to
  ABCDEFGHI

I chose a single calico fabric for most of Patty's skin, with a slightly darker piece (H2) for her neck to give her chin more definition. Patty's blouse is cut from a large-scale print, with darker parts of the print chosen for the bodice and a lighter part for the sleeve.

To further separate the bodice from the sleeve, I quilted each separately using a variegated cotton thread. Notice the quilted ripples in the orange fabric at the nose of the iron.

And a Yard of This One

Your fabric stash is your palette. Most quilters acquire a collection of fabrics over time, either deliberately or as scraps from previous projects. My stash is composed of commercially printed and a few purchased hand-dyed fabrics. While almost all of my fabrics are cotton, they may have been originally designed for use in clothing or home décor rather than quilting.

I use the whole range of these fabrics in all of my quilts. The prints and patterns add texture and complexity as well as references to the many ways we use fabrics in our lives.

Enlarge this block 210% to a 10" x 19" rectangle, see page 8. The size suggested is the minimum practical size. To make it easier, make it bigger.

During construction, press the seam allowances in the direction indicated by the arrows on the Piecing Diagram.

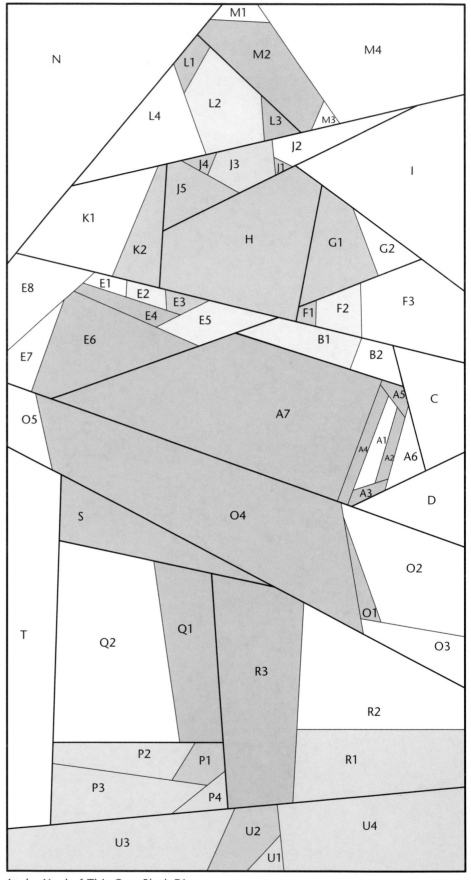

And a Yard of This One *Block Diagram*

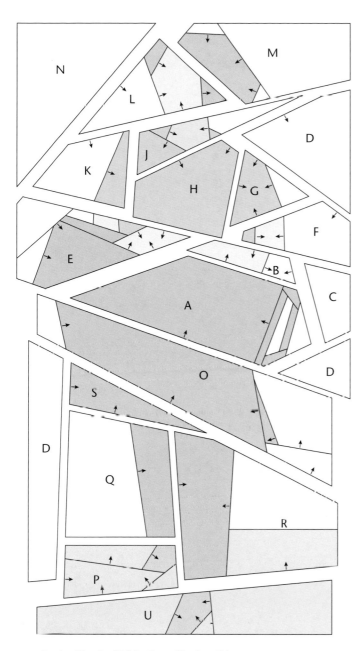

And a Yard of This One *Piecing Diagram*

Sew:
A1 to A2 to A3 to A4 to A5 to A6 to A7
B1 to B2 to A to C to D
E1 to E2 to E3 to E4 to E5 to E6 to E7 to E8 to
  ABCD
F1 to F2 to F3
G1 to G2 to F to H to I
J1 to J2 to J3 to J4 to J5 to FGHI
K1 to K2 to FGHIJ
L1 to L2 to L3 to L4
M1 to M2 to M3 to M4 to L to FGHIJK to
  ABCDE to N
O1 to O2 to O3 to O4 to O5 to
  ABCDEFGHIJKLMN
P1 to P2 to P3 to P4
Q1 to Q2 to P, R1 to R2 to R3 to PQ to S to T
U1 to U2 to U3 to U4 to PQRST to
  ABCDEFGHIJKLMNO

One of the white fabrics used in the wall is part of a shirt from a rummage sale; the large plaid is an Indian Madras. I prefer the Madras plaids because of their scale and wonderful mix of colors, values, and varying line widths, rather than the smaller and more restrained plaids designed for quiltmakers.

The bolt of fabric in Rose's arms is a hand-dye with enough variation to show off the different segments of the piecing. I used a little strip of printed letters from a selvage to make the label on the cardboard core of the bolt.

Rose's skin is a print with trees and dots in it. You can see a larger piece of this in Choosing Fabrics for Skin on page 22. The fabric for her face was fussy cut to include a suggestion of eyes, not as successfully as I would have liked. I used a section of the same fabric with a darker stripe to create the shadow on her neck.

This Is an Interesting Fabric
Libby, Mary, and Anne

Every quiltmaker sees fabric differently. It's fascinating how different and unique each person's selections can be. And it's equally fascinating how one fabric will be used quite differently by different quiltmakers. To me, an "interesting" fabric is usually not pretty in a conventional sense. It isn't one you would choose for a dress or draperies.

I find that my students make the most progress in expanding their fabric vocabulary in week-long workshops. The students share with each other as need arises. Sometimes a fabric that the student would *never* buy herself is just the thing she needs to complete her quilt.

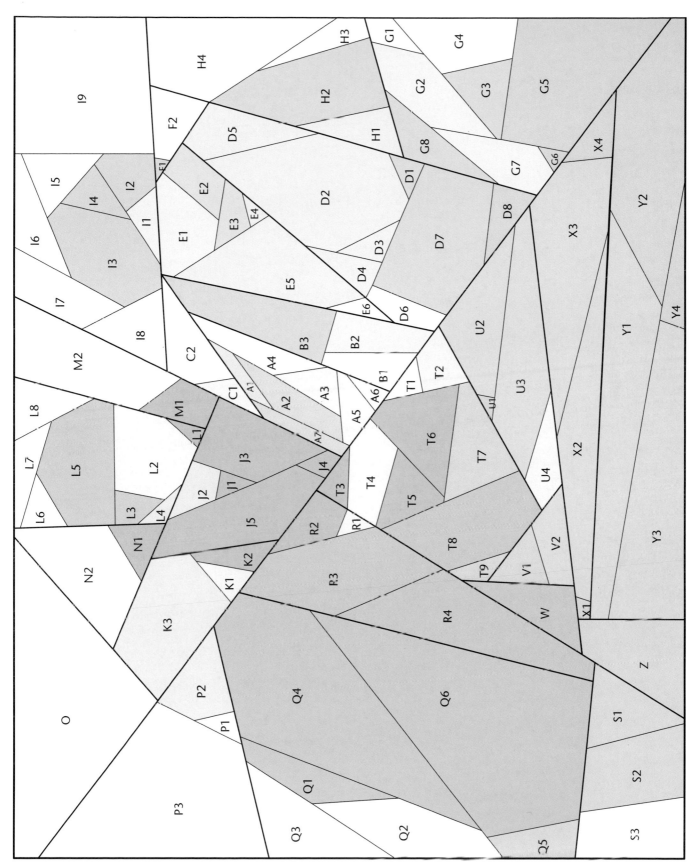

This Is an Interesting Fabric *Block Diagram*

Enlarge this block 243% to a 21¼" x 17" rectangle, see page 8. The size suggested is the minimum practical size. To make it easier, make it bigger.

During construction, press the seam allowances in the direction indicated by the arrows on the Piecing Diagram.

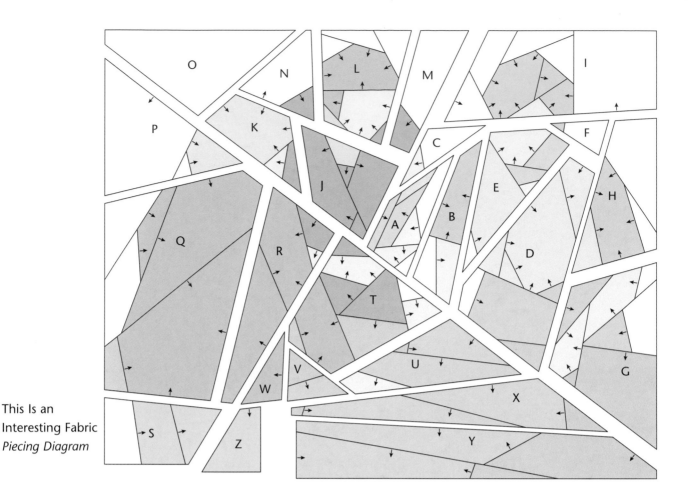

This Is an
Interesting Fabric
Piecing Diagram

Sew:
A1 to A2
A3 to A4 to A(1,2) to A5 to A6 to A7
B1 to B2 to B3 to A
C1 to C2 to AB
D1 to D2 to D3 to D4 to D5
D6 to D7 to D8 to D(1,2,3,4,5)
E1 to E2 to E3 to E4 to E5 to E6 to D to ABC
F1 to F2 to ABCDE
G1 to G2
G3 to G4 to G(1,2) to G5
G6 to G7 to G(1,2,3,4,5) to G8
H1 to H2 to H3 to H4 to G to ABCDEF
I1 to I2
I3 to I4 to I(1,2) to I5 to I6 to I7 to I8 to I9 to
   ABCDEFGH

J1 to J2 to J3
J4 to J5 to J(1,2,3), K1 to K2 to K3 to J
L1 to L2 to L3 to L4 to L5 to L6 to L7 to L8
M1 to M2 to L
N1 to N2 to LM to JK to O to ABCDEFGHI
P1 to P2 to P3, Q1 to Q2 to Q3 to Q4
Q5 to Q6 to Q(1,2,3,4) to P
R1 to R2 to R3 to R4 to PQ
S1 to S2 to S3 to PQR, T1 to T2
T3 to T4 to T5 to T6 to T7 to T(1,2) to T8 to T9
U1 to U2 to U3 to U4 to T
V1 to V2 to TU to W
X1 to X2 to X3 to X4
Y1 to Y2
Y3 to Y4 to Y(1,2) to X to Z to TUVW to PQRS to
   ABCDEFGHIJKLMNO

Here we have Libby with her back toward us, Mary with a quilting book in her arm, and Anne unfolding a bolt on a cutting table. The striped fabric is a hand-woven from Guatemala. If you plan to use a striped fabric, draw an arrow for the direction of the stripe on the back of each freezer paper piece, then align the

stripe with the arrow when ironing the template on the back of the fabric.

I used two different pink fabrics for Anne's dress to define the separate parts. See Adding Pieces to the Quilted Surface on page 27 for ideas on adding extra fabrics to the table.

Fondling Fabric

Have you ever watched a group of quilters in a fabric store? They need to touch all the fabrics. At quilt shows, it's almost impossible to keep viewers from handling the quilts in spite of ropes and warning signs.

When I teach my design classes, I have my students begin by drawing and planning their quilt on paper. They are often unfamiliar with this process, and the anxiety level tends to be high. As soon as they start to unpack and spread out their fabric hoards, everyone begins to relax. The tactile quality of the materials is a very important reason why so many people enjoy making quilts.

Nina is fondling a large-scale print fabric from Australia. Notice how you can see the folds and facets in the cloth by the discontinuities of the print from one piece to the next. If I had used a plain fabric instead, Nina's fabric would lack the feeling of lively motion this print shows off so well.

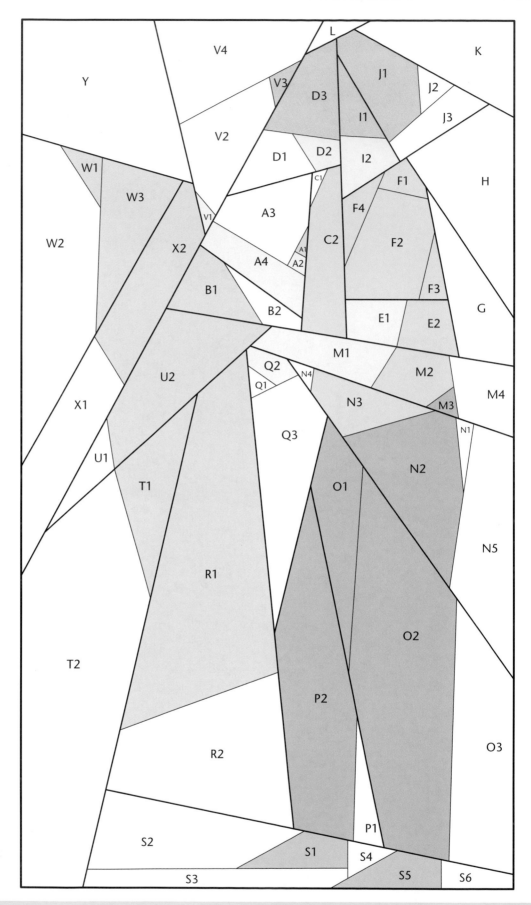

Fondling Fabric
Block Diagram

Enlarge this block 214% to an 11" x 19⅜" rectangle, see page 8. The size suggested is the minimum practical size. To make it easier, make it bigger.

During construction, press the seam allowances in the direction indicated by the arrows on the Piecing Diagram.

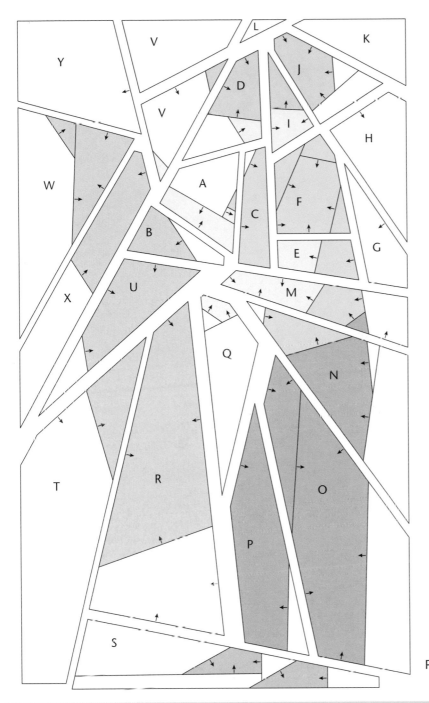

Fondling Fabric *Piecing Diagram*

Sew:
A1 to A2 to A3 to A4
B1 to B2 to A
C1 to C2 to AB
D1 to D2 to D3 to ABC
E1 to E2
F1 to F2 to F3 to F4 to E to G to H
I1 to I2
J1 to J2 to J3 to I to EFGH to K
ABCD to EFGHIJK to L
M1 to M2 to M3 to M4
N1 to N2 to N3 to N4 to N5

O1 to O2 to O3
P1 to P2 to O
Q1 to Q2 to Q3 to OP to N to M
R1 to R2 to MNOPQ
S1 to S2 to S3 to S4 to S5 to S6 to MNOPQR
T1 to T2 to MNOPQRS
U1 to U2 to MNOPQRST to ABCDEFGHIJKL
V1 to V2 to V3 to V4
W1 to W2 to W3
X1 to X2 to W to Y to V
ABCDEFGHIJKLMNOPQRSTU to VWXY

Rhoda Cohen chose a checked fabric for Nina to fling in the air in this version of the block. The breaks in the check pattern show off the folds in the fabric. The background pieces were all cut from the same fabric, but selected to be yellow/red at the top and greener at the floor level. The darker values in this background allowed Rhoda to use a light value stripe for Nina's pants.

Fondling Fabric,
pieced by Rhoda Cohen

Folding Up the Leftovers Judy

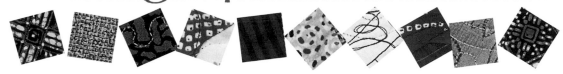

I must confess that when I am deep into the construction of a quilt, my sewing room becomes awash with fabric. I often find myself tossing fabrics into the air, trying to find the one I had a minute ago. The fabrics often land in unexpected and unplanned juxtapositions, which sometimes find their way into the quilt. These are combinations that I might not have discovered if I worked in a more orderly manner.

Folding fabric at the end of a project becomes a necessary task to avoid drowning completely in a sea of scraps and to prepare for the next quilt. It's also a time to look at each piece again, smoothing and folding and tucking it away, while unwinding from the creative frenzy.

For the yoke of Judy's quilted dress, I used a geometric print that looked like patchwork. I tried to visualize the direction that the fabric grain would run in an actual dress as I cut a narrow stripe for the rest of the dress. Mark the stripe direction on the back of the freezer paper pieces so you can easily place them in the right direction on the back of the striped fabric.

Many quiltmakers like to collect colorful socks as well as fabric. I just love Judy's green and dotted pair.

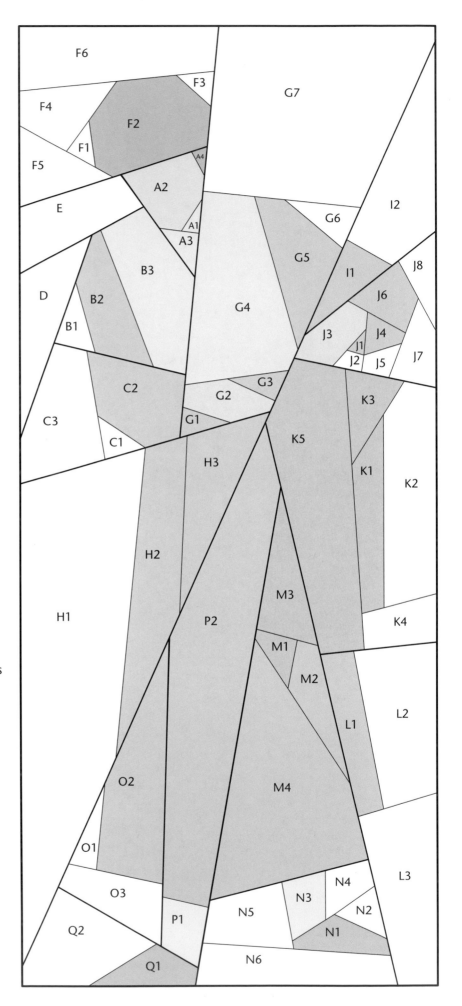

Folding Up the Leftovers
Block Diagram

Enlarge this block 185% to an 8" x 18½" rectangle, see page 8. The size suggested is the minimum practical size. To make it easier, make it bigger.

During construction press the seam allowances in the direction indicated by the arrows on the Piecing Diagram.

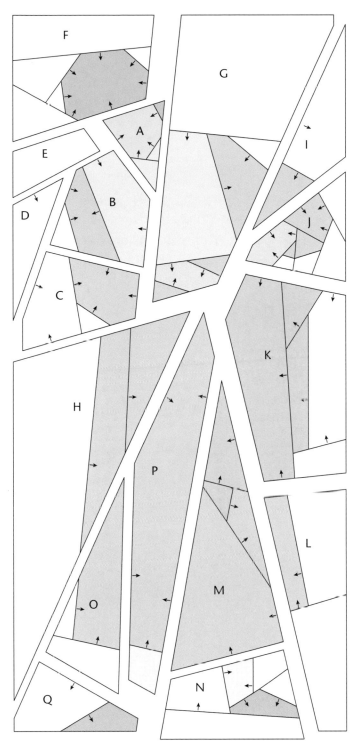

Folding Up the Leftovers *Piecing Diagram*

Sew:
A1 to A2 to A3 to A4
B1 to B2 to B3
C1 to C2 to C3 to B to D to E to A
F1 to F2 to F3 to F4 to F5 to F6 to ABCDE
G1 to G2 to G3 to G4 to G5 to G6 to G7 to
  ABCDEF
H1 to H2 to H3 to ABCDEFG
I1 to I2
J1 to J2 to J3
J4 to J5 to J(1,2,3) to J6 to J7 to J8 to I
K1 to K2 to K3 to K4 to K5 to IJ
L1 to L2 to L3 to IJK
M1 to M2 to M3 to M4
N1 to N2
N3 to N4 to N(1,2) to N5 to N6 to M
O1 to O2 to O3
P1 to P2 to O
Q1 to Q2 to OP to MN to IJKL to ABCDEFGH

Choosing a Palette of Fabrics
Dorothy and Harriet

Choosing a set of fabrics (a palette) for a new quilt is best done with the actual fabrics. Find a place to work with good lighting, ideally the kind of lighting that will be shining on the finished quilt. Work from your stash, or with the fabrics in your favorite quilt shop, and spread out your selections to see how they look as a group. Pay attention to the mix of patterns in the fabrics as well as the colors. You may get lots of offers of advice in fabric selection, but this is your quilt. Make choices that please your taste and reflect your style.

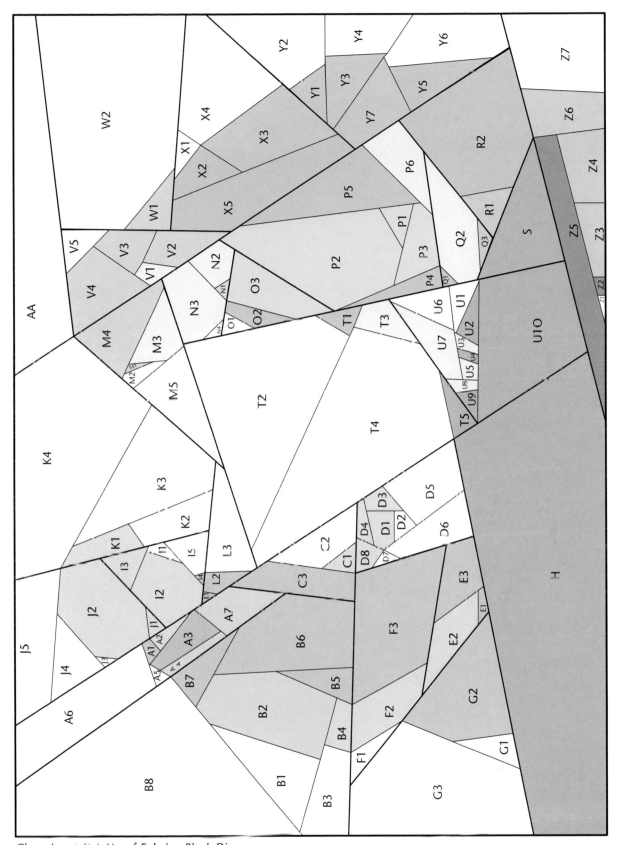

Choosing a Palette of Fabrics *Block Diagram*

Enlarge this block 210% to an 18" x 13" rectangle, see page 8. The size suggested is the minimum practical size. To make it easier, make it bigger.

During construction, press the seam allowances in the direction indicated by the arrows on the Piecing Diagram.

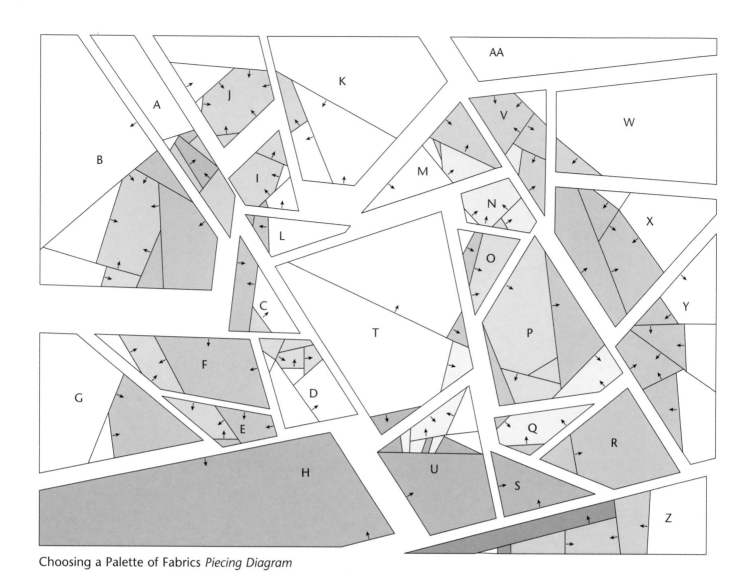

Choosing a Palette of Fabrics *Piecing Diagram*

Sew:
A1 to A2 to A3 to A4 to A5 to A6 to A7
B1 to B2
B3 to B4 to B(1,2) to B5 to B6 to B7 to B8 to A
C1 to C2 to C3 to AB
D1 to D2 to D3 to D4 to D5 to D6
D7 to D8 to D(1,2,3,4,5,6)
E1 to E2 to E3
F1 to F2 to F3 to E to D
G1 to G2 to G3 to DEF to H to ABC
I1 to I2 to I3
I4 to I5 to I(1,2,3)
J1 to J2 to J3 to J4 to J5 to I
K1 to K2 to K3 to K4 to IJ
L1 to L2 to L3 to IJK
M1 to M2 to M3 to M4 to M5 to IJKL
N1 to N2 to N3 to N4
O1 to O2 to O3 to N

P1 to P2 to P3 to P4 to P5 to P6 to NO
Q1 to Q2 to Q3 to NOP
R1 to R2 to NOPQ to S
T1 to T2
T3 to T4 to T(1,2) to T5
U1 to U2 to U3 to U4 to U5
U6 to U7 to U(1,2,3,4,5) to U8 to U9 to U10 to T
  to NOPQRS to IJKLM
V1 to V2 to V3 to V4 to V5
W1 to W2, X1 to X2, X3 to X4 to X(1,2) to X5 to
  W to V to AA
Y1 to Y2
Y3 to Y4
Y5 to Y6 to Y7, Y(1,2) to Y(3,4) to Y(5,6,7) to
  VWX(AA) to IJKLMNOPQRSTU to ABCDEFG
Z1 to Z2 to Z3 to Z4 to Z5 to Z6 to Z7 to
  ABCDEFGHIJKLMNOPQRSTUVWXY(AA)

Choosing a Palette of Fabrics *with added fabric pieces*

On the finished block, I placed pieces of fabric on the table and fused them in place. I left the edges raw, and folded one edge a little, so it looks like Harriet (on the right) is moving it. You can also cut and arrange the pieces on the table to look like pieces of a quilt top. See Adding Pieces to the Quilted Surface on page 27.

Pinning on a Design Wall Natalie

Natalie is stretching as high as she can to pin pieces for her quilt on the design wall. Many quilt artists today arrange elaborate designs on a vertical surface where they can stand back to see the overall effect, rather than planning a traditional block and sewing many identical blocks as quiltmakers often did in the past. In fact, many contemporary quilts are planned as wall art rather than bedspreads, although many of the techniques and fabrics used are often similar.

I included chunks of colorful fabrics in the background piecing to represent the quilt Natalie is working on. These fabrics look like pieces of patchwork to me. See Choosing Fabrics for Quilts-in-Progress on page 26 for other ideas to personalize your block.

I fussy cut Natalie's jeans from a piece of Chinese indigo-dyed shibori to give her a pair of pockets. You can further embellish this block by sewing some pins to hold the quilt pieces to the design wall. Make the pins from long stitches of a metallic thread and add some glass seed beads for their heads.

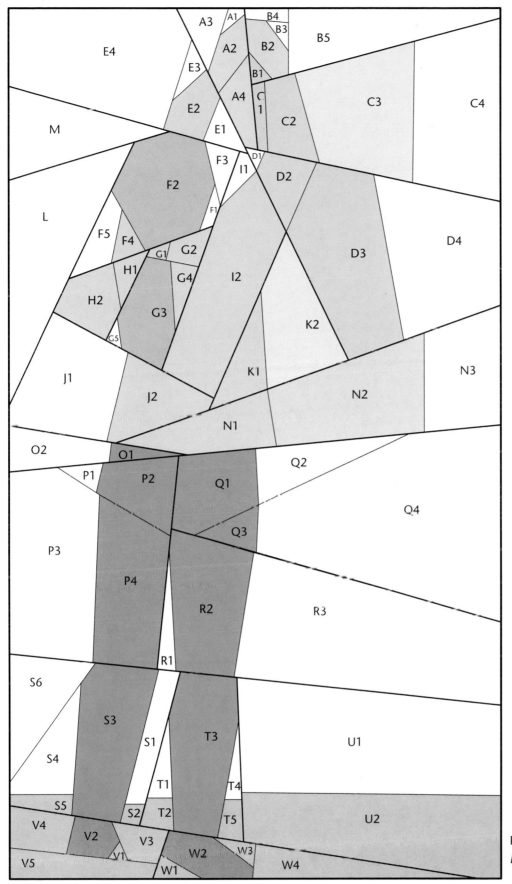

Block Diagram labels: A3, A1, B4, B3, A2, B2, B5, E4, E3, A4, B1, C1, C3, C4, E2, E1, C2, M, F3, I1, D1, D2, F2, F1, D3, D4, L, F5, F4, G1, G2, G4, I2, H1, H2, G3, K2, G5, K1, N3, J1, J2, N1, N2, O2, O1, Q2, P1, P2, Q1, Q4, P3, Q3, P4, R2, R3, R1, S6, S3, S1, T3, U1, S4, T1, T4, S5, T2, T5, U2, V4, V2, V3, W2, W3, W4, V5, V1, W1

Pinning on a Design Wall
Block Diagram

Enlarge this block 214% to an 11" x 19½" rectangle, see page 8. The size suggested is the minimum practical size. To make it easier, make it bigger.

During construction, press the seam allowances in the direction indicated by the arrows on the Piecing Diagram.

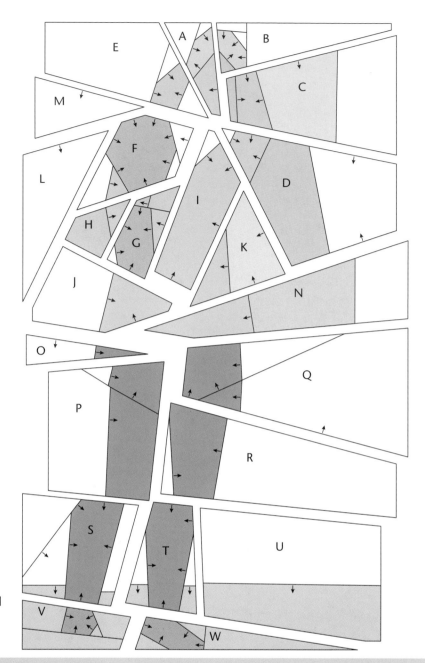

Pinning on a Design Wall
Piecing Diagram

Sew:
A1 to A2 to A3 to A4
B1 to B2 to B3 to B4 to B5
C1 to C2 to C3 to C4 to B to A
D1 to D2 to D3 to D4 to ABC
E1 to E2 to E3 to E4
F1 to F2 to F3
F4 to F5 to F(1,2,3)
G1 to G2
G3 to G4 to G5 to G(1,2)
H1 to H2 to G to F
I1 to I2 to FGH
J1 to J2 to FGHI
K1 to K2 to FGHIJ to L to M to E to ABCD
N1 to N2 to N3 to ABCDEFGHIJKLM

O1 to O2 to ABCDEFGHIJKLMN
P1 to P2
P3 to P4 to P(1,2)
Q1 to Q2
Q3 to Q4 to Q(1,2)
R1 to R2 to R3 to Q to P to ABCDEFGHIJKLMNO
S1 to S2 to S3
S4 to S5 to S(1,2,3) to S6
T1 to T2 to T3
T4 to T5 to T(1,2,3) to S
U1 to U2 to ST
V1 to V2 to V3 to V4 to V5
W1 to W2 to W3 to W4 to V to STU to
    ABCDEFGHIJKLMNOPQR

For her version of the block, Rhoda Cohen chose stripey jeans and a flowery shirt of dark fabrics to make Natalie's silhouette stand out against the light wall fabric. Rhoda carefully cut the fabric for Natalie's hair to be shaded light on the top and darker underneath.

Pinning on a Design Wall,
pieced by Rhoda Cohen

Auditioning Fabric

Pamela is also working on her design wall, holding up a piece of blue checked fabric to see if she'd like to use a piece of it with the other fabrics she's already pinned in place. You can only see the top of her curly hair as she studies the effect.

I love indigo blue and decided to use it for Pamela's clothes and in her quilt. The pieces for the quilt are cut from three Japanese cottons printed with fans and patchwork. I was careful to choose fabric for quilt pieces F3 and F4 that had areas of lighter colors because they are next to Pamela's head, F1. Her brown hair is the same value as the blues in these quilt fabrics and would have blended with them. See Relative Values in Fabrics on page 24.

Pamela has on a dark-purple watchband, or maybe a wrist pincushion. She'll straighten up and stand back when she gets this piece of checked fabric pinned in place, to see how she likes it from a distance.

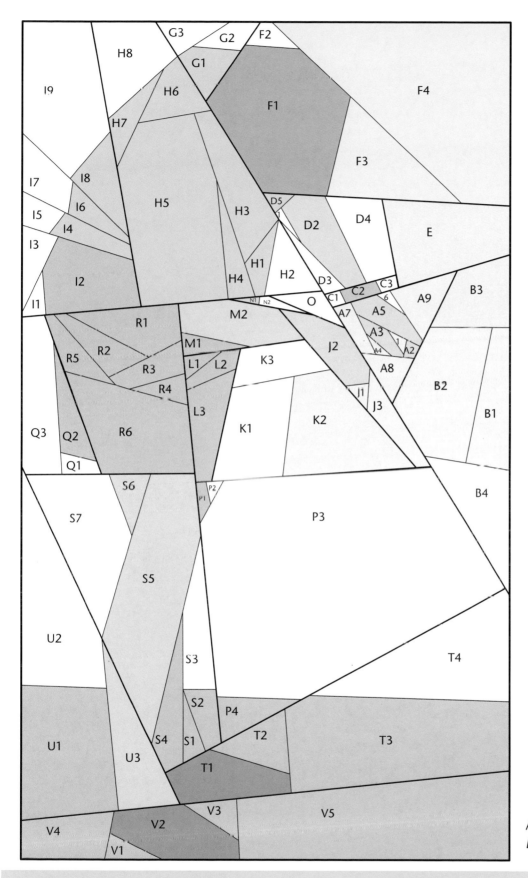

Auditioning Fabric
Block Diagram

Enlarge this block 244% to a 12½" x 21⅜" rectangle, see page 8. The size suggested is the minimum practical size. To make it easier, make it bigger.

During construction, press the seam allowances in the direction indicated by the arrows on the Piecing Diagram.

Auditioning Fabric *Piecing Diagram*

Sew:
A1 to A2 to A3 to A4 to A5 to A6 to A7 to A8 to A9
B1 to B2 to B3 to B4 to A
C1 to C2 to C3
D1 to D2 to D3 to D4 to D5 to C to E to AB
F1 to F2 to F3 to F4 to ABCDE
G1 to G2 to G3 to ABCDEF
H1 to H2 to H3
H4 to H5 to H(1,2,3) to H6 to H7 to H8
I1 to I2 to I3
I4 to I5 to I(1,2,3)
I6 to I7
I8 to I9 to I(6,7) to I(1,2,3,4,5) to H
J1 to J2 to J3

K1 to K2 to K3
L1 to L2 to L3 to K
M1 to M2 to KL to J
N1 to N2 to JKLM to O
P1 to P2 to P3 to P4 to JKLMNO
R1 to R2 to R3 to R4 to R5 to R6
Q1 to Q2 to Q3 to R
S1 to S2 to S3 to S4 to S5
S6 to S7 to S(1,2,3,4,5) to QR to JKLMNOP to HI
T1 to T2 to T3 to T4 to HIJKLMNOPQRS
U1 to U2 to U3 to HIJKLMNOPQRST
V1 to V2 to V3 to V4 to V5 to HIJKLMNOPQRSTU
   to ABCDEFG

Auditioning Fabric, *pieced by Rhoda Cohen*

Rhoda Cohen interpreted this block using a very different selection of fabrics. The dark hair, shorts, floor, and two pieces of the quilt make a nice balance. Rhoda fussy cut an ombré plaid of green, blue, and purple to make each piece of Pamela's shirt a slightly different shade. The bright green for Pam's watchband is a terrific color choice.

Sharing the Process

Cynthia, Vickie, and Norah

Cynthia, Vickie, and Norah (in order from left to right) are taking a break and sharing some thoughts about fabric choices in a workshop. Almost every quilter I have met is a really nice person. I love teaching five-day workshops and getting to know the students. Many quilters find these long workshops a great place to make new quilting friends as well as learn new skills. Workshops are also a great place to see many different quilts come alive on the walls.

I used four different yellow fabrics in Vickie's sweater to add some shading. Norah's colorful shirt is cut from a tropical-fish fabric. In cutting this fabric, I tried to position the black background of the print in places where it would make shadows under her arms. Write on the back of the freezer paper pieces where you want the darks to be to help you in ironing the paper templates to the right parts of the print.

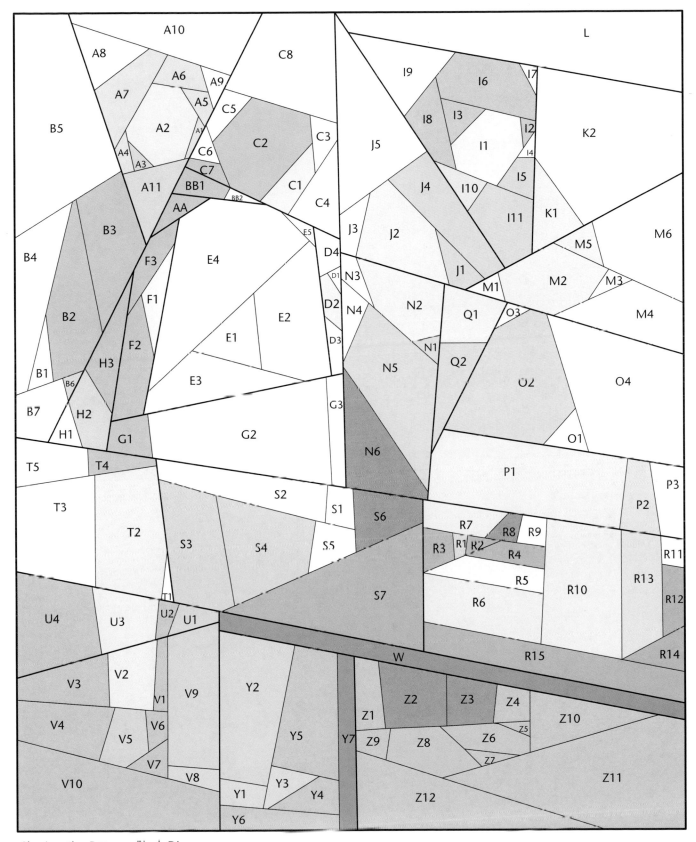

Sharing the Process *Block Diagram*

Enlarge this block 333% to a 23¼" x 28⅜" rectangle, see page 8. The size suggested is the minimum practical size. To make it easier, make it bigger.

During construction, press the seam allowances in the direction indicated by the arrows on the Piecing Diagram.

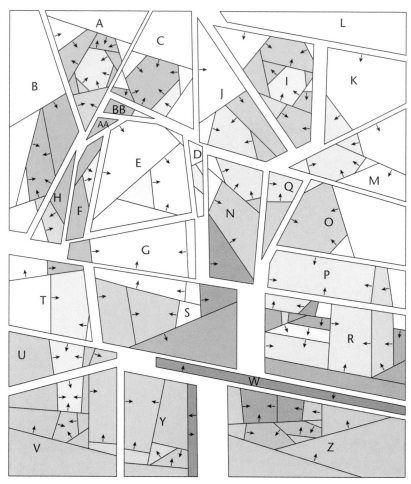

Sharing the Process
Piecing Diagram

Sew:

A1 to A2 to A3 to A4 to A5 to A6 to A7 to A8 to A9 to A10 to A11

B1 to B2 to B3 to B4 to B5

B6 to B7 to B(1,2,3,4,5) to A

C1 to C2 to C3 to C4 to C5

C6 to C7 to C(1,2,3,4,5) to C8

D1 to D2 to D3 to D4

E1 to E2 to E3 to E4 to E5 to D

F1 to F2 to F3 to DE to AA

BB1 to BB2 to DEF(AA) to C

G1 to G2 to G3 to CDEF(AA,BB)

H1 to H2 to H3 to CDEFG(AA, BB) to AB

I1 to I2 to I3

I4 to I5 to I(1,2,3) to I6 to I7 to I8 to I9

I10 to I11 to I(1,2,3,4,5,6,7,8,9)

J1 to J2 to J3 to J4 to J5

K1 to K2 to I to L to J

M1 to M2 to M3 to M4

M5 to M6 to M(1,2,3,4) to IJKL

N1 to N2 to N3

N4 to N5 to N(1,2,3) to N6

O1 to O2 to O3 to O4

P1 to P2 to P3 to O

Q1 to Q2 to OP to N to IJKLM to ABCDEFGH(AA,BB)

R1 to R2 to R3

R4 to R5 to R(1,2,3) to R6

R7 to R8 to R9 to R(1,2,3,4,5,6) to R10

R11 to R12 to R13 to R14 to R(1,2,3,4,5,6,7,8,9,10) to R15

S1 to S2

S3 to S4 to S5 to S(1,2) to S6 to S7

T1 to T2 to T3

T4 to T5 to T(1,2,3) to S to R

U1 to U2 to U3 to U4

V1 to V2 to V3

V4 to V5 to V6 to V7 to V(1,2,3)

V8 to V9 to V(1,2,3,4,5,6,7) to V10 to U

Y1 to Y2

Y3 to Y4 to Y5 to Y(1,2) to Y6 to Y7

Z1 to Z2 to Z3 to Z4

Z5 to Z6 to Z7 to Z8 to Z9 to Z(1,2,3,4) to Z10 to Z11 to Z12 to Y to W to UV to RST to ABCDEFGHIJKLMNOP(AA,BB)

Sharing the Process with added fabrics

A workshop room is always a mass of fabric once the quilters get their supplies out. I added piles of fabric to the tables and floors, and scraps everywhere. See Adding Pieces to the Quilted Surface on page 27.

Design Workshop

Karen, Lucy, and Janet

Here's Karen again in the foreground, still hand sewing while Lucy and Janet collaborate on a quilt pinned up on the design wall. A Featherweight sits ready to go on a nearby table, along with piles of fabric (see page 79).

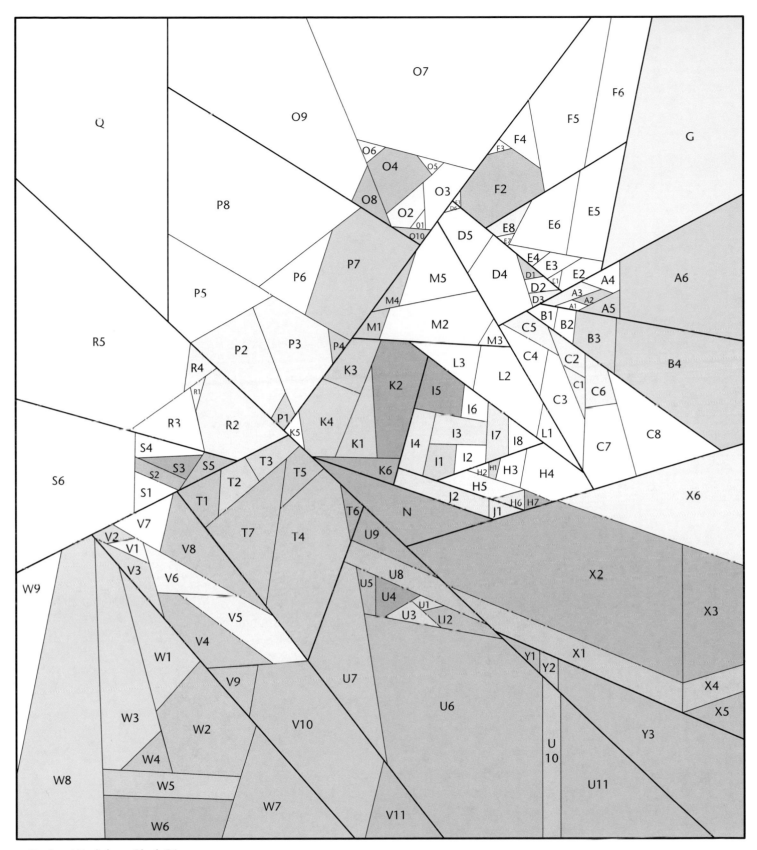

Design Workshop *Block Diagram*

Enlarge this block 323% to a 24⅜" x 27½" rectangle, see page 8. The size suggested is the minimum practical size. To make it easier, make it bigger.

During construction, press the seam allowances in the direction indicated by the arrows on the Piecing Diagram.

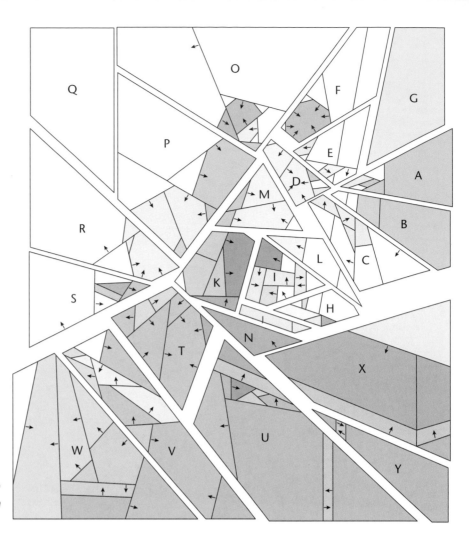

Design Workshop
Piecing Diagram

Sew:
A1 to A2 to A3 to A4 to A5 to A6
B1 to B2 to B3 to B4
C1 to C2
C3 to C4 to C5 to C(1,2)
C6 to C7 to C8 to C(1,2,3,4,5) to B to A
D1 to D2 to D3 to D4 to D5 to D6
E1 to E2 to E3 to E4
E5 to E6
E7 to E8
E(1,2,3,4) to E(5,6) to E(7,8)
F1 to F2 to F3 to F4 to F5 to F6 to E to D to G
  to ABC
H1 to H2 to H3 to H4
H5 to H6 to H7 to H(1,2,3,4)
I1 to I2 to I3 to I4
I5 to I6 to I(1,2,3,4) to I7 to I8 to H
J1 to J2 to HI
K1 to K2
K3 to K4 to K5 to K(1,2) to K6 to HIJ
L1 to L2 to L3 to HIJK
M1 to M2 to M3
M4 to M5 to M(1,2,3) to HIJKL to N to ABCDEFG

O1 to O2 to O3
O4 to O5 to O6 to O(1,2,3) to O7
O8 to O9 to O(1,2,3,4,5,6,7) to O10
P1 to P2 to P3 to P4 to P5
P6 to P7 to P8 to P(1,2,3,4,5) to O to Q to
  ABCDEFGHIJKLMN
R1 to R2 to R3
R4 to R5 to R(1,2,3)
S1 to S2 to S3 to S4 to S5 to S6 to R
T1 to T2 to T3
T4 to T5 to T6 to T7 to T(1,2,3)
U1 to U2 to U3 to U4 to U5 to U6 to U7 to U8 to U9
  to U10 to U11 to T
V1 to V2 to V3
V4 to V5 to V6 to V(1,2,3)
V7 to V8 to V(1,2,3,4,5,6)
V9 to V10 to V11 to V(1,2,3,4,5,6,7,8) to TU
W1 to W2
W3 to W4 to W(1,2) to W5 to W6 to W7 to W8 to
  W9 to TUV to RS
X1 to X2, X3 to X4 to X5 to X(1,2) to X6, Y1 to Y2
  to Y3 to X to ABCDEFGHIJKLMNOPQ to RSTUVW

To convey the wonderful confusion of fabrics Lucy and Janet are considering, I added stacks of fabric to the pieced block after the quilting was done. I wanted to keep their edges raw and add them in an unstructured way, as a contrast to the fabrics that were pieced into the block. See Adding Pieces to the Quilted Surface on page 27.

Design Workshop *with added fabric*

Rhoda Cohen's version of the *Design Workshop* block uses a darker fabric on the upper left wall, with a light area around Lucy and Janet. I especially like the balance this gives to the scene. The quilt-in-progress is multiple pieces of the same leafy fabric, an effective choice for this section of the block.

Design Workshop, *pieced by Rhoda Cohen*

Hand Quilting on a Big Frame

Jane

Jane is hand quilting on a big frame, the kind many quiltmakers can sit around to work together. For fun, make several of these blocks and arrange them in a row as though your pieced quilters were all working on the same quilt—kind of like a quilters chorus line. Give them different clothing and hair colors, and even reverse one block to make a left-handed quilter.

To piece Jane's sweater, I chose two batiks of very similar colors. This allowed her left sleeve to show up against her body. I cut the pieces for Jane's face and hand from the same leaf-printed fabric, and fussy cut the fingers to get some shading along their edges. I think the right hand came out amazingly well. When you make your block, be sure to cut Jane's neck, B2 and E2, and wrist, P1 and R1, from a darker part of the fabric, or another darker fabric, to place them in shadow.

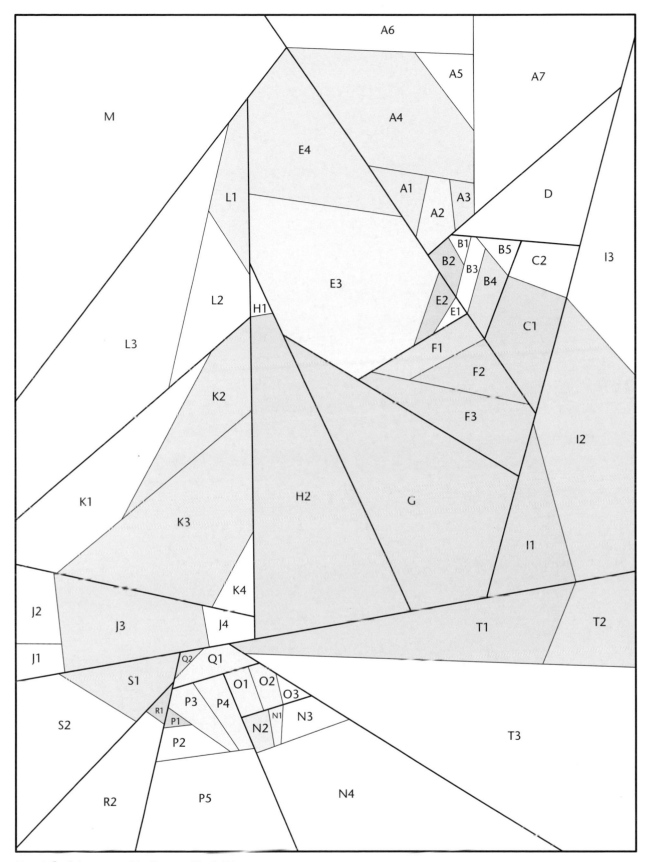

Hand Quilting on a Big Frame *Block Diagram*

Enlarge this block 200% to a 13" x 17½" rectangle, see page 8. The size suggested is the minimum practical size. To make it easier, make it bigger.

During construction, press the seam allowances in the direction indicated by the arrows on the Piecing Diagram.

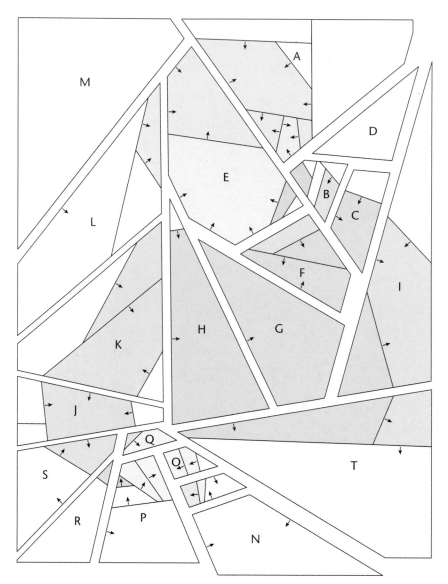

Hand Quilting on a Big Frame *Piecing Diagram*

Detail of Jane's hand and the patchwork quilt

Sew:
A1 to A2 to A3 to A4 to A5 to A6 to A7
B1 to B2 to B3 to B4 to B5
C1 to C2 to B to D to A
E1 to E2 to E3 to E4
F1 to F2 to F3 to E to G
H1 to H2 to EFG
I1 to I2 to I3
J1 to J2 to J3 to J4

K1 to K2 to K3 to K4 to J
L1 to L2 to L3 to JK to EFGH to M to ABCD to I
O1 to O2 to O3
N1 to N2 to N3 to N4 to O
P1 to P2 to P3 to P4 to P5 to NO to Q1 to Q2
S1 to S2
R1 to R2 to S to NOPQ
T1 to T2 to T3 to NOPQRS to ABCDEFGHIJKLM

I made a small piece of patchwork for the quilt in the frame by combining the yellow polka-dot fabric (see page 21) with a blue fabric. I fussy cut the polka-dot fabric to get red quarter circles in the squares. I arranged them similar to a Mill Wheel pattern and cut

the patchwork into the eight pieces required for the block (N3, N4, O3, P2, P5, R2, S2, T3, J1). I did not worry about the discontinuities in the Mill Wheel pattern that developed. I like the way it shows off the piecing in the block.

Hand Quilting in a Hoop Chris

Quilters hand quilt in many different ways. Some work on a big frame, some like a round or oval hoop, and others prefer no hoop at all.

For the quilt in the hoop, I used a piece of Marimekko fabric that looked almost like patchwork. See Choosing Fabrics for Quilts-in-Progress on page 26 for other ideas. Chris's sweater is a hand-woven ikat fabric cut in different directions to make the body of the sweater different from the sleeves.

I used a brown leafy print for Chris's hair and drew arrows on the freezer paper (I2, J2, L4) to make sure it grew in the right direction. I hand quilted the quilt and machine quilted the figure and the background. I also embroidered a needle and thread in Chris's right hand.

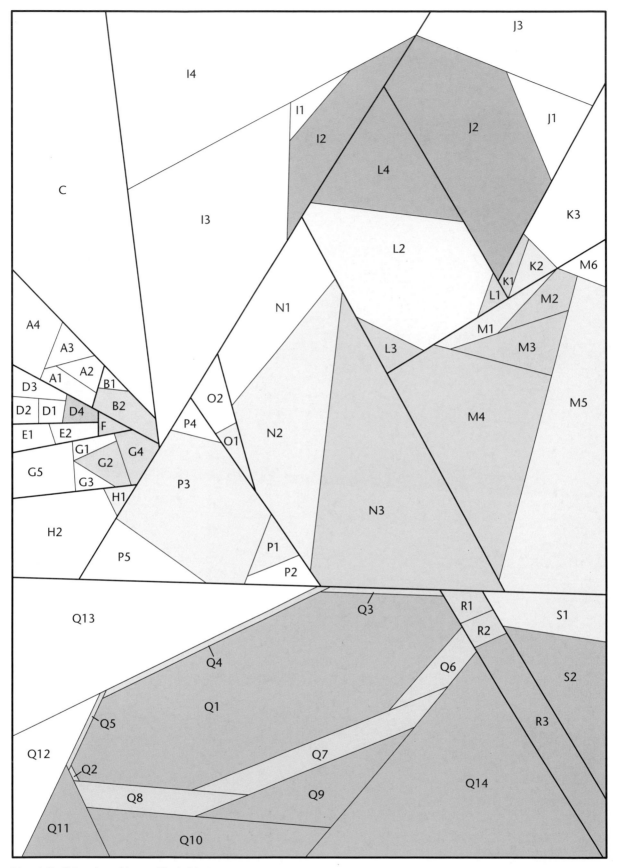

Hand Quilting in a Hoop *Block Diagram*

Enlarge this block 230% to a 14¼" x 20¼" rectangle, see page 8. The size suggested is the minimum practical size. To make it easier, make it bigger.

During construction, press the seam allowances in the direction indicated by the arrows on the Piecing Diagram.

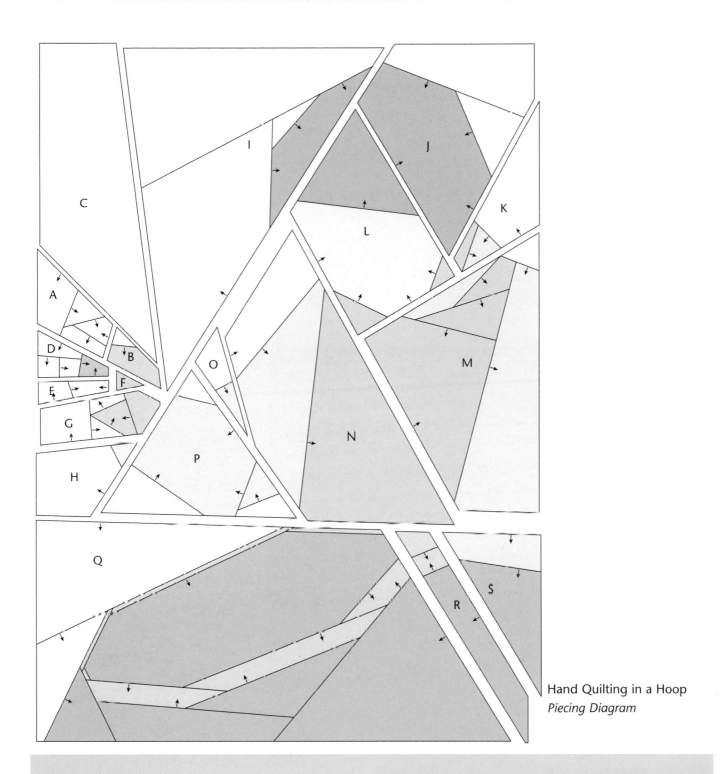

Hand Quilting in a Hoop
Piecing Diagram

Sew:
A1 to A2 to A3 to A4
B1 to B2 to A to C
D1 to D2 to D3 to D4
E1 to E2 to D to F
G1 to G2 to G3 to G4 to G5 to DEF to ABC
H1 to H2 to ABCDEFG
I1 to I2 to I3 to I4 to ABCDEFGH
J1 to J2 to J3
K1 to K2 to K3 to J
L1 to L2 to L3 to L4 to JK

M1 to M2 to M3 to M4 to M5 to M6 to JKL
N1 to N2 to N3 to JKLM
O1 to O2 to JKLMN
P1 to P2 to P3 to P4 to P5 to JKLMNO
ABCDEFGHI to JKLMNOP
Q1 to Q2 to Q3 to Q4 to Q5 to Q6 to Q7 to Q8 to
 Q9 to Q10 to Q11 to Q12 to Q13 to Q14
R1 to R2 to R3 to Q
S1 to S2 to QR
ABCDEFGHIJKLMNOP to QRS

Detail of Chris's right hand

Chris's skin is a shaded batik fabric with little ferns. The palm of her right hand and the thumb, pieces F, G2, G4, and B2, were cut from a darker part of the batik, and her fingers, A1, D1, E2, and G1, were cut from a lighter section.

Hand Quilting in a Hoop: Oak Leaf and Cherries, *19" x 25½"*

A traditional red and green Oak Leaf and Cherries block that I made twenty-five years ago inspired a second version of *Hand Quilting in a Hoop.* I framed this block with simple borders to create a small wallhanging.

Machine Quilting

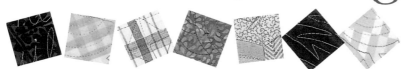

Free-motion machine quilting is like drawing with the sewing machine, but the sewing machine stays in one place while the quilter moves the quilt. This is a bit like making a drawing by moving the paper rather than the pencil. It takes a bit of practice to master.

Kathy is machine quilting with dropped feed dogs and a darning foot. Notice that I drew the darning foot with the machine quilting.

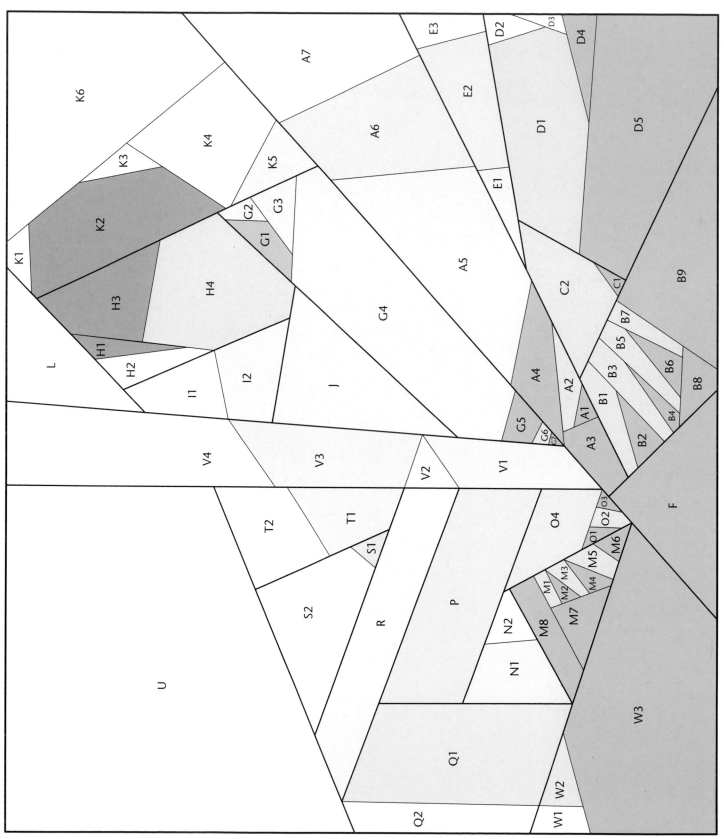

Machine Quilting *Block Diagram*

Enlarge this block 176% to a 13" x 15" rectangle, see page 8. The size suggested is the minimum practical size. To make it easier, make it bigger.

During construction, press the seam allowances in the direction indicated by the arrows on the Piecing Diagram.

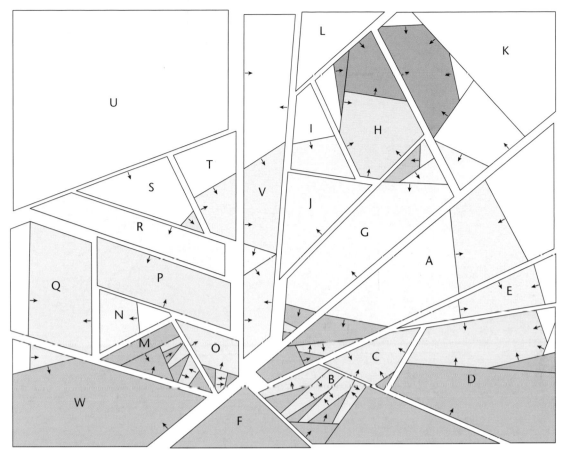

Machine Quilting *Piecing Diagram*

Sew:

A1 to A2 to A3 to A4 to A5 to A6 to A7
B1 to B2 to B3 to B4 to B5 to B6 to B7 to B8 to B9
C1 to C2
D1 to D2 to D3 to D4 to D5 to C to B
E1 to E2 to E3 to BCD to A to F
G1 to G2 to G3 to G4 to G5 to G6 to G7
H1 to H2 to H3 to H4
I1 to I2 to H to J to G
K1 to K2 to K3 to K4 to K5 to K6 to GHIJ to L

M1 to M2 to M3 to M4 to M5 to M6 to M7 to M8
N1 to N2 to M
O1 to O2 to O3 to O4 to MN to P to Q1 to Q2 to R
S1 to S2
T1 to T2 to S to MNOPQR to U
V1 to V2 to V3 to V4 to MNOPQRSTU
W1 to W2 to W3 to MNOPQRSTUV to GHIJKL to
ABCDEF

Piece M5 represents the index and middle finger of Kathy's right hand. I used a line of machine quilting to separate them visually. If you quilt with gloves on, you can add gloves by making pieces A2, B1, B3, B5, B7, C2, M1, M3, M5, and G6 from glove-colored fabric.

I cut Kathy's shirt from two coordinated Marimekko fabrics, a patchwork stripe for the sleeves and yoke, and a patchwork check for the bodice. Notice the cuff, E2, on Kathy's left sleeve. I selected the lightest part of the fabric to go next to the darkest part of the bodice fabric, E1.

The quilt that Kathy is working on is made from another Marimekko fabric with a bit of a border print. Her generic sewing machine can be detailed with quilting, embroidered details, or other surface techniques. I drew a spool on the machine with machine quilting stitches, and a handle, thread cutter, and plug as well.

Meandering (see page 91) shows this block cropped to make a striking graphic image for use as a repeated block.

Repeated Block Quilts

Meandering

Meandering, *34" x 21½", Paulette Peters*

To make a stronger and simpler graphic image, I cropped *Machine Quilting* down to focus in on Kathy's hands. Used as a repeated block, it creates a strong but simple image with unlimited possibilities.

My friend Paulette Peters made the *Meandering* quilt from this block. She used four blocks, each 14½" x 7½". The inner borders of the quilt are 1" wide (cut 1½"). The top and bottom outer borders are 2¾" wide (cut 3¼") and the side outer borders are 2" wide (cut 2½").

Enlarge this block 153% to a 7½" x 14½" rectangle, see page 8. The size suggested is the minimum practical size. To make it easier, make it bigger.

During construction, press the seam allowances in the direction indicated by the arrows on the Piecing Diagram.

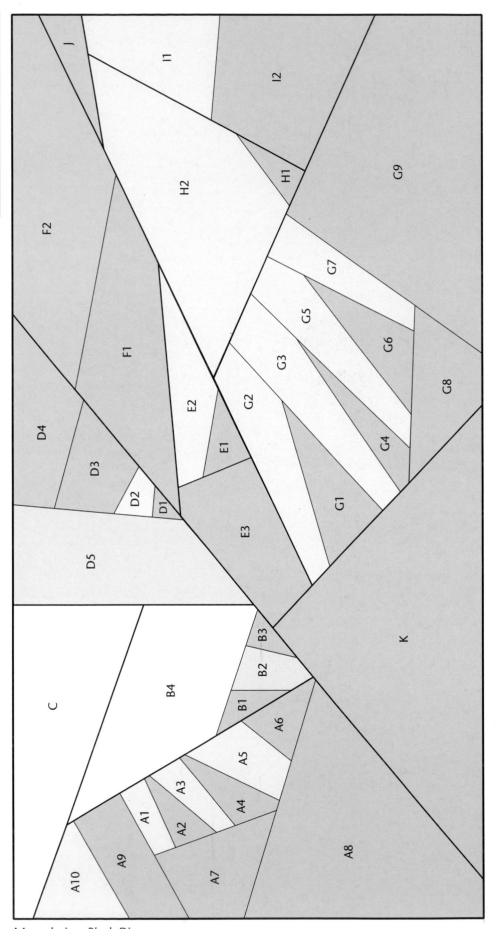

Meandering *Block Diagram*

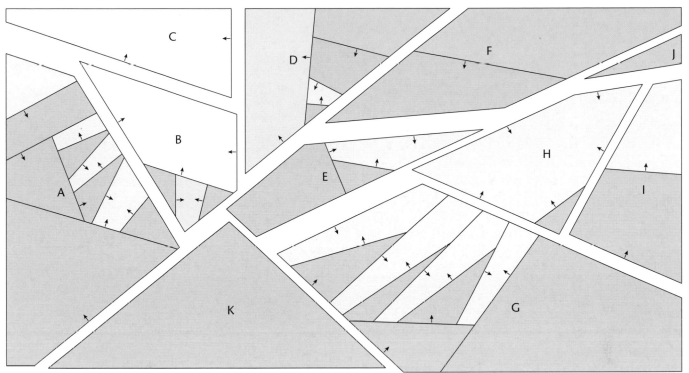

Meandering *Piecing Diagram*

Sew:
A1 to A2 to A3 to A4 to A5 to A6 to A7 to A8 to A9
 to A10
B1 to B2 to B3 to B4 to A to C
D1 to D2 to D3 to D4 to D5 to ABC
E1 to E2 to E3

F1 to F2 to E
G1 to G2 to G3 to G4 to G5 to G6 to G7 to G8
 to G9
H1 to H2
I1 to I2 to H to J to G to EF to K to ABCD

Meandering *block*

Making Repeated Blocks: *Paulette
made four freezer paper patterns, one for each
block, rather than reusing the patterns. To make
sure that all the pieces of a single traced block were
sewn back together again, she labeled each block
using a different colored pencil. She felt the freezer
paper blocks might not be traced or cut apart
exactly the same for each block. See Repeated
Blocks on page 14.*

Whizzy Whackers

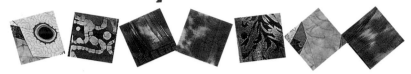

This is another quilt made by Paulette Peters. This one uses a repeated block cropped from *Rotary Cutting.*

Paulette used twelve blocks, each 8½" x 13". The inner borders are 1" wide (cut 1½"). The outer borders are 2½" wide (cut 3"). She cut the knobs for the rotary cutters from a dotted print and machine appliquéd them to the pieced blocks.

See *Meandering* on page 91 for tips on making templates for repeated blocks.

Whizzy Whackers, 41" x 44½", Paulette Peters

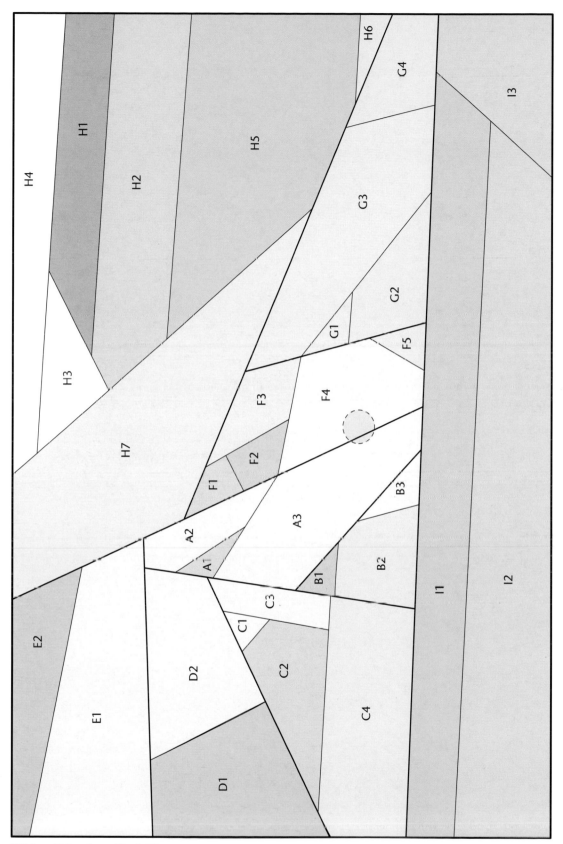

Whizzy Whackers *Block Diagram*

Enlarge this block 151% to an 8½" x 13" rectangle, see page 8. The size suggested is the minimum practical size. To make it easier, make it bigger.

During construction, press the seam allowances in the direction indicated by the arrows on the Piecing Diagram.

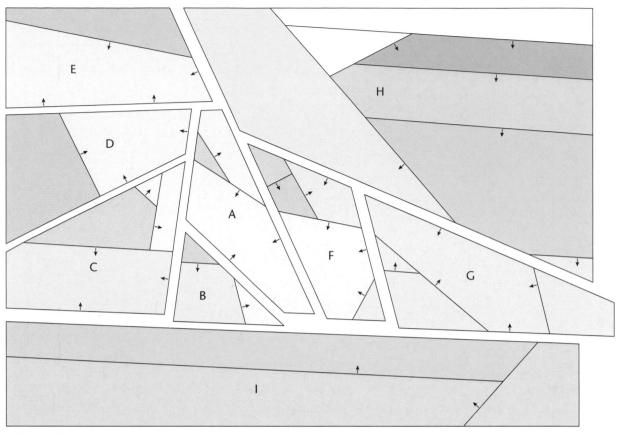

Whizzy Whackers *Piecing Diagram*

Sew:
A1 to A2 to A3
B1 to B2 to B3 to A
C1 to C2 to C3 to C4
D1 to D2 to C to AB
E1 to E2 to ABCD

F1 to F2 to F3 to F4 to F5
G1 to G2 to G3 to G4 to F
H1 to H2 to H3 to H4 to H5 to H6 to H7 to FG
 to ABCDE
I1 to I2 to I3 to ABCDEFGH

Whizzy Whackers
block

Spinning Featherweights

Focusing in on the little black Featherweight and Nancy's hands from *Sewing on a Featherweight* makes a block that works well as a repeated image. Paulette Peters made this charming wall-hanging with four blocks arranged in pinwheel fashion around a central square.

Spinning Featherweights, 36½" x 36½", Paulette Peters

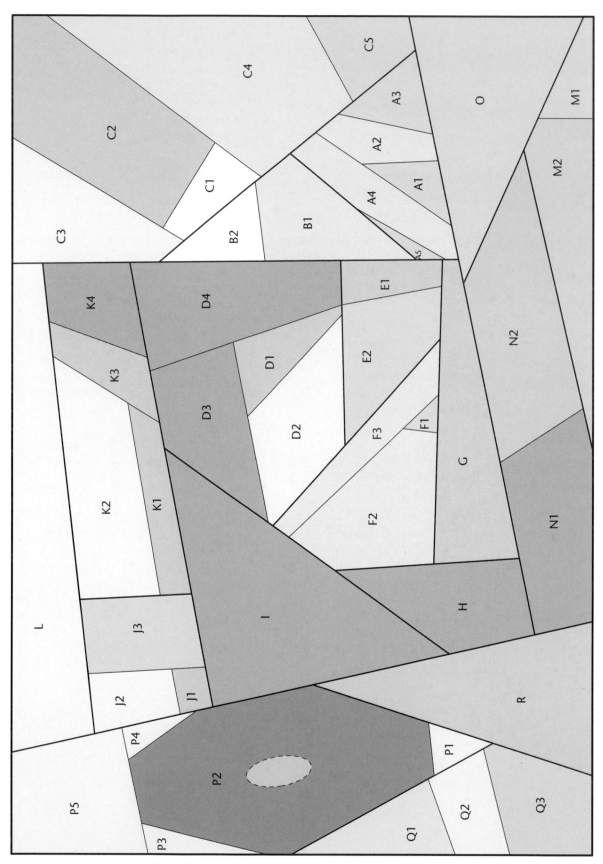

Spinning Featherweights *Block Diagram*

Enlarge this block 206% to an 18" x 12½" rectangle, see page 8. The size suggested is the minimum practical size. To make it easier, make it bigger.

During construction, press the seam allowances in the direction indicated by the arrows on the Piecing Diagram.

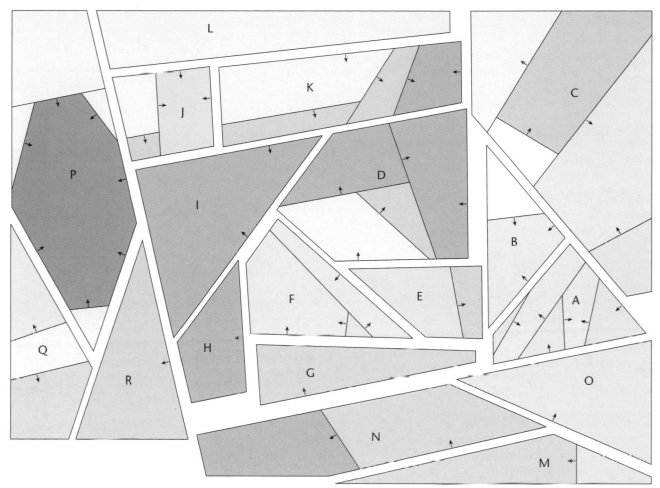

Spinning Featherweights *Piecing Diagram*

Sew:
A1 to A2 to A3 to A4 to A5
B1 to B2 to A
C1 to C2 to C3 to C4 to C5 to AB
D1 to D2 to D3 to D4
E1 to E2 to D
F1 to F2 to F3 to DE to G to H to I
J1 to J2 to J3
K1 to K2 to K3 to K4 to J to L to DEFGHI to ABC
N1 to N2
M1 to M2 to N to O to ABCDEFGHIJKL
P1 to P2 to P3 to P4 to P5
Q1 to Q2 to Q3 to P to R to ABCDEFGHIJKLMNO

Spinning Featherweights *block*

Each block has a finished size of 18" x 12½" with a central square of 5½" x 5½" (cut 6" x 6"). The inner borders are pieced of 1" black and colored squares (cut 1½" x 1½"). The outer border is 2½" wide (cut 3").

Sewing the completed blocks together with this central square will require a partial seam (see page 109).

Small Wallhangings and Samplers

Small Wallhangings from Single Blocks

Any block from this book can make a fun small wallhanging. I chose two of the blocks to frame as examples.

I like to include references to traditional quilting, so I chose Sawtooth borders for this example. The triangles that form the Sawtooth edge around the *Machine Quilting* block were cut from some of the same fabrics that were used in the block, and a few additional ones. I randomly scattered the colors to complement the colors in the pieced block. In this way, the border frames the piece without confining it.

Machine Quilting Wallhanging, *23" x 19"*

Auditioning Fabric Wallhanging, *17" x 25"*

For *Auditioning Fabric Wallhanging,* I took my cues for the border from the fabrics in the pieced block. I cut strips of the quilt fabrics for the upper right corner, extending Pamela's quilt into the border. Then I used other indigo prints to complete the frame. Again, my aim was to frame the piece well but not imprison it. The insertion of a light fabric in the right border lets some air in.

Setting a Scene

In planning a scene, you will find that most of the blocks in this book pair together well. I chose two blocks, both showing views of a workshop, to blend together in a wallhanging as though they were part of the same scene.

Sharing the Process

Design Workshop

When constructing each block, I chose the same fabrics for the floors, tables, and walls to give some consistency. I placed the blocks near each other and slid the right one up a little so the figures seemed in the right perspective. The three figures in the left block were larger than the two in the right block (Lucy and Janet), but smaller than Karen in the chair (if she stood up).

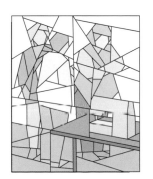 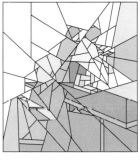

Placing the figures in perspective

The blocks were also different sizes, so I added some strips to make them fit together. As with the little wall-hangings on pages 101–102, I like to include traditional quilt references and especially like Sawtooth borders. The triangles in the border were a way to integrate the two blocks.

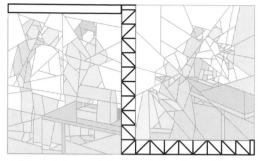

Adding strips and Sawtooth borders with spacers to join the blocks

I chose to cut triangles that would finish 3" inches on a side. Because the block dimensions were not an even multiple of 3, I added some narrow spacer strips on each side and in the strip between the blocks, to make the borders come out evenly.

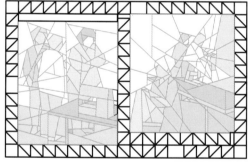

Adding Sawtooth borders

When I cut the triangles for the borders, I included some fabrics used for the table and floor, and some from other fabrics used in the two blocks. I played with the placement until the blocks seemed to meld, and finished the borders with bright corner squares.

The Scene Wallhanging before adding scraps

design workshop

The Scene Wallhanging, *56" x 36"*

Using the Blocks to Make a Sampler

Any number of blocks from this book can be set together to make a sampler-style quilt. I chose thirteen blocks—all different sizes—and added extra fabrics and borders to complete the design.

Sampler Quilt,
82" x 61"

I find this style of quilt fits together most easily if I make the blocks and then plan the setting on graph paper.

1 Make the blocks. To simplify the math, you may want to trim the blocks so that the finished size of each will be an even number of inches. That is, rather than use a block that is an odd finished size, trim it to make the finished block an even number of inches. For example, if the block is 13⅞" x 9¾", trim it to 13½" x 9½" so that it finishes at 13" x 9".

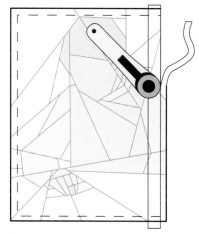

Trim the blocks to an even number of inches (finished size).

2 Lay the blocks out on the floor or table, or pin them to the design wall, shifting them around until you are pleased with the placement. Because the blocks are different sizes, you will have gaps between them here and there.

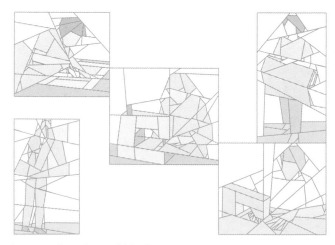

Arrange the trimmed blocks.

3 On graph paper, make a small scale drawing of your planned layout. Cut little paper rectangles to scale for each block, match them with the grid on the graph paper, and glue them in place.

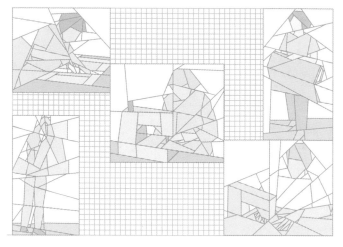

Scale drawing of sampler on graph paper

4 Fill in the spaces between the pieced blocks with rectangles and squares as needed. You will be able to count the squares in the grid on the graph paper to get the finished size of these additional filler pieces. Remember to add seam allowances when scaling up and cutting these extra filler pieces.

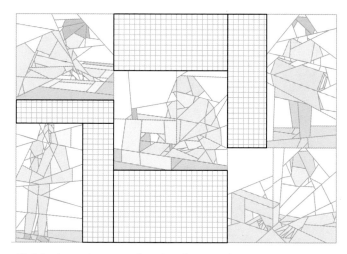

Finished graph paper drawing for sampler

5 Sew the blocks together. Depending on how you lay out the blocks, the sewing may have some "puzzle" pieces. Sew these with partial seams as needed (see next page for instructions on partial seams).

Evening Up Blocks

A sampler is easier to plan and sew if the blocks are all the same size. The easiest way to do this is to add strips to the sides of the blocks until all the blocks are the same size.

Sharyn Craig, fellow quilter, author, and teacher, calls these strips "coping strips"—what a great name! Once the blocks are the same size, you can set the blocks together edge to edge or with sashing in any standard quilt set.

Add strips to even the sizes of several blocks.

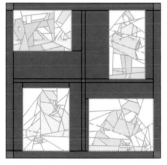 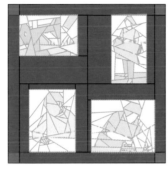 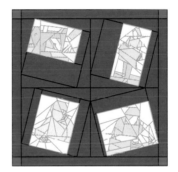

Various sets with equal-sized blocks

Partial Seam Assembly

Seam 1 (partial)

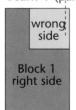 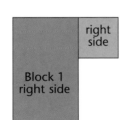

Seam 2

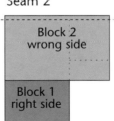 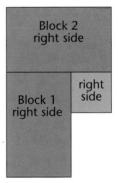

Seam 3

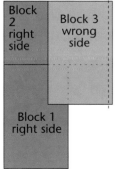 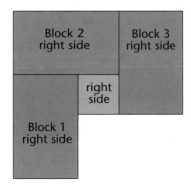 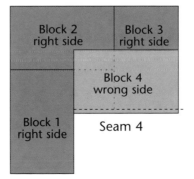 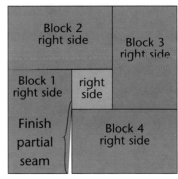

Seam 4

Finish partial seam

Fabric Choices

The thirteen blocks I used in my sampler have light backgrounds with multicolored figures. I wanted to use multicolored fabrics to fill in between the blocks, so I chose large-scale prints to add interest and break up the geometry. This also lets the blocks flow together. A solid fabric, especially a solid dark fabric, for these extra pieces would isolate the blocks from each other, confining the figures in little cells.

The fabrics I chose included the two Japanese fabrics shown on page 21, two fabrics with squares and rectangles of clear bright colors resembling patchwork, and a large-scale, flowery print with a black background that included many of the colors in the pieced blocks.

The flowery print was once part of a skirt that a quilter friend found in a thrift shop several years ago. She shared it with me and I used it all up in this quilt, piecing the leftover scraps with yellow squares of another fabric to get enough for an inner border. It looks *better* with those yellow squares than it would have if I had used more of the skirt fabric itself.

The outer border is all that's left of a fabric I designed for Kona Bay in 1993. The little abstract trees sparkle against the black background of this fabric and keep it from overwhelming the quilt as a solid black fabric would have done. The little bits of tan, white, and blue in the tree fabric tie it to the colors in the rest of the quilt as well.

Detail of skirt fabric, upper right corner of the Sampler Quilt

Some of the spacing pieces include fussy-cut squares of the hands from the two Japanese prints, in one case pieced into a Nine-Patch.

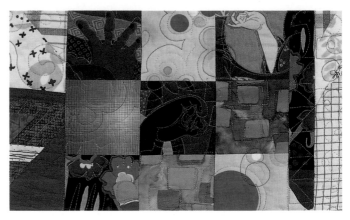

Nine-Patch with fussy-cut hands

Conclusion

The world of quilts and quilters is a wonderful place; a funny, colorful, and caring community. This book is dedicated to celebrating quilters in their many and various forms. I hope it encourages you to try your hand at designing figures as well.

Happy quilting!

About the Author

Ruth B. McDowell is an internationally known professional quilt artist, teacher, lecturer, and author. She has made over 300 quilts during the last two decades. Her quilts have been seen in many solo shows, as well as in dozens of magazines and books. Ruth resides in Winchester, Massachusetts.

Photo by Amy Marson

Visit Ruth's Website at
www.ruthbmcdowell.com

Other Books by Ruth B. McDowell

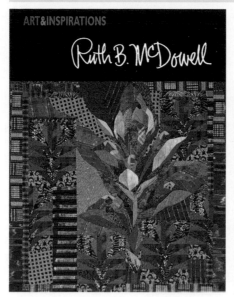

Art & Inspirations: Ruth B. McDowell
(Out of Print)

Pieced Vegetables

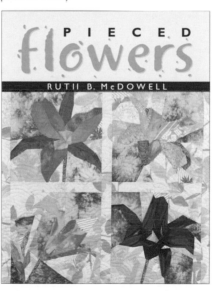

Pieced Flowers

Piecing: Expanding the Basics

For more information, write for a free catalog:

C&T Publishing, Inc.

P.O. Box 1456

Lafayette, CA 94549

(800) 284-1114

Email: ctinfo@ctpub.com

Website: www.ctpub.com

For quilting supplies:

Cotton Patch Mail Order

3405 Hall Lane, Dept. CTB

Lafayette, CA 94595

(800) 835-4418

(925) 283-7883

Email: quiltusa@yahoo.com

Website: www.quiltusa.com

Note: Fabrics used in the quilts shown may not be currently available since fabric manufacturers keep most fabrics in print for only a short time.

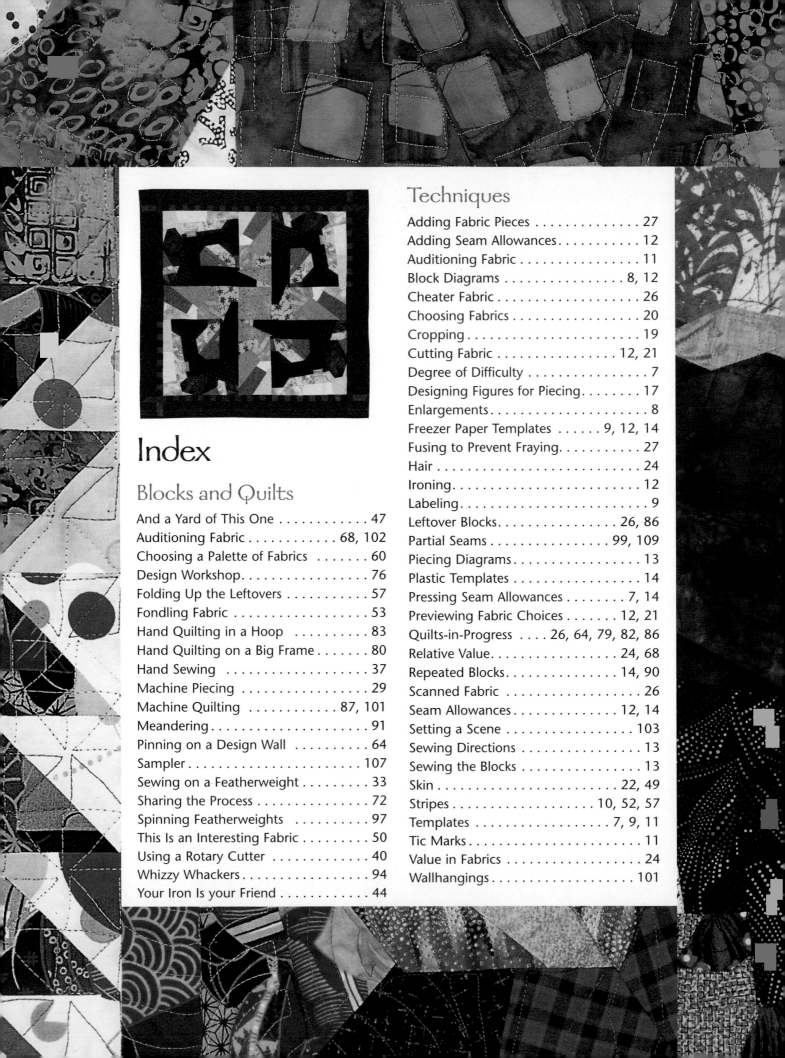

Index

Blocks and Quilts

And a Yard of This One 47
Auditioning Fabric 68, 102
Choosing a Palette of Fabrics 60
Design Workshop. 76
Folding Up the Leftovers 57
Fondling Fabric 53
Hand Quilting in a Hoop 83
Hand Quilting on a Big Frame 80
Hand Sewing 37
Machine Piecing 29
Machine Quilting 87, 101
Meandering. 91
Pinning on a Design Wall 64
Sampler 107
Sewing on a Featherweight 33
Sharing the Process 72
Spinning Featherweights 97
This Is an Interesting Fabric 50
Using a Rotary Cutter 40
Whizzy Whackers. 94
Your Iron Is your Friend 44

Techniques

Adding Fabric Pieces 27
Adding Seam Allowances. 12
Auditioning Fabric 11
Block Diagrams 8, 12
Cheater Fabric 26
Choosing Fabrics 20
Cropping. 19
Cutting Fabric 12, 21
Degree of Difficulty 7
Designing Figures for Piecing. 17
Enlargements. 8
Freezer Paper Templates 9, 12, 14
Fusing to Prevent Fraying. 27
Hair 24
Ironing. 12
Labeling. 9
Leftover Blocks. 26, 86
Partial Seams 99, 109
Piecing Diagrams. 13
Plastic Templates 14
Pressing Seam Allowances 7, 14
Previewing Fabric Choices 12, 21
Quilts-in-Progress 26, 64, 79, 82, 86
Relative Value. 24, 68
Repeated Blocks. 14, 90
Scanned Fabric 26
Seam Allowances. 12, 14
Setting a Scene 103
Sewing Directions 13
Sewing the Blocks 13
Skin 22, 49
Stripes 10, 52, 57
Templates 7, 9, 11
Tic Marks 11
Value in Fabrics 24
Wallhangings. 101